CW00971178

OSPREY COMBAT AIRCRAFT • 22

MITSUBISHI TYPE 1 *RIKKO* 'BETTY'

UNITS OF WORLD WAR 2

SERIES EDITOR: TONY HOLMES

OSPREY COMBAT AIRCRAFT • 22

MITSUBISHI TYPE 1 *RIKKO* 'BETTY'
UNITS OF WORLD WAR 2

Osamu Tagaya

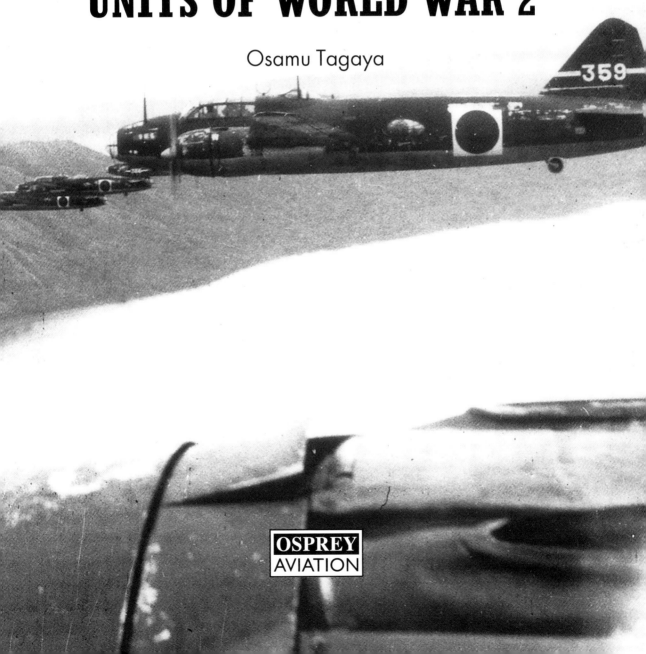

OSPREY
AVIATION

Front cover
On 2 December 1941 (just five days prior to the Japanese attack on Pearl Harbor and the invasion of South-east Asia) the Royal Navy's *Force Z* arrived in Singapore, Britain's bastion in the Far East. Commanded by Rear Adm Sir Tom Phillips, and centred around one of the Royal Navy's newest battleships in HMS *Prince of Wales*, as well as the old, but combat-seasoned, battlecruiser HMS *Repulse*, *Force Z* represented the most formidable naval obstacle facing Japan's plans for the invasion of Malaya and the capture of Singapore. Between them, these two warships outgunned Japanese surface units committed to the Malayan operation. *Force Z* had to be stopped at all cost, for if it got within range of the lightly protected invasion convoy then untold damages could be inflicted.

Near midday on 10 December 1941, Type 96 (G3M2 'Nell') and Type 1 (G4M1 'Betty') Land-based Attack Aircraft of the Imperial Navy's 22nd *Koku Sentai* (Air Flotilla), operating at extreme range from their bases near Saigon, in French Indochina, caught the two British capital ships off Kuantan, on the east coast of Malaya. When the 26 Type 1s of the Kanoya *Kokutai* arrived on the scene at around 1220, the ships had already survived the attention of 32 of the older Type 96 aircraft from the Genzan and Mihoro *Kokutais*. Both vessels had sustained some damage from the 'Nells', *Prince of Wales* in particular having lost its ability to steer, but neither warship was in any immediate danger of sinking. Indeed, the battlecruiser *Repulse* was still very much in full fighting trim, the vessel's armoured decks easily withstanding a single superficial bomb hit, and all 15 torpedoes so far fired at it having been successfully avoided. The fate of both capital ships now rested in the hands of the new Type 1s of the Kanoya *Kokutai*.

Unable to steer, *Prince of Wales* was quickly struck by four torpedoes from the Kanoya's 1st and 2nd *Chutais* and sank about an hour later. By then a single torpedo had also finally struck *Repulse* , although the 'old warrior' was still in good working order. The 3rd *Chutai* now concentrated on the stubborn battlecruiser.

First published in Great Britain in 2001 by Osprey Publishing
Elms Court, Chapel Way, Botley, Oxford, OX2 9LP
E-mail: info@ospreypublishing.com

© 2001 Osprey Publishing Limited

All rights reserved. Apart from any fair dealing for the purpose of private study, research, criticism or review, as permitted under the Copyright, Design and Patents Act, 1988, no part of this publication may be reproduced, stored in a retrieval system, or transmitted in any form or by any means, electronic, electrical, chemical, mechanical, optical, photocopying, recording or otherwise, without prior written permission. All enquiries should be addressed to the publisher.

ISBN 1 84176 082 X

Edited by Tony Holmes
Page design by TT Designs, T & B Truscott
Cover Artwork by Iain Wyllie
Aircraft Profiles and Scale Drawings by Mark Styling
Origination by Grasmere Digital Imaging, Leeds, UK
Printed through Bookbuilders, Hong Kong

01 02 03 04 05   10 9 8 7 6 5 4 3 2 1

EDITOR'S NOTE
To make this best-selling series as authoritative as possible, the Editor would be interested in hearing from any individual who may have relevant photographs, documentation or first-hand experiences relating to aircrews, and their aircraft, of the various theatres of war. Any material used will be credited to its original source. Please write to Tony Holmes at 10 Prospect Road, Sevenoaks, Kent, TN13 3UA, Great Britain, or by e-mail at: tony.holmes@osprey-jets.freeserve.co.uk

ACKNOWLEDGEMENTS
The Author wishes to express his deepest thanks to the following individuals for their invaluable assistance in the preparation of this volume, and in their generous provision of excellent photographs: Lawrence J Hickey, Robert C Mikesh, Shigeru Nohara, James F Lansdale, James I Long, Yoshio Tagaya, Edward M Young, Ichiro Mitsui of Bunrindo K K, Minoru Akimoto, Dana Bell, David Pluth and Tom Hall.

For a catalogue of all Osprey Publishing titles please contact us at:

Osprey Direct UK, PO Box 140, Wellingborough, Northants NN8 4ZA, UK
E-mail: **info@ospreydirect.co.uk**

Osprey Direct USA, c/o Motorbooks International, 729 Prospect Ave, PO Box 1, Osceola, WI 54020, USA
E-mail: **info@ospreydirectusa.com**

Or visit our website: **www.ospreypublishing.com**

This specially-commissioned cover painting by Iain Wyllie shows the aircraft of Lt Haruki Iki, leader of the Kanoya's 3rd *Chutai*, as it 'hurdles' HMS *Repulse* following its attack. Iki's bomber suffered 17 hits but survived the terrific anti-aircraft barrage thrown up by the battlecruiser. His two wingmen were not so lucky, both falling in mushroom balls of flame, but not before they had released their torpedoes. All three weapons found their mark on the port side of the ship, whilst the 3rd *Chutai's* remaining flights also contributed a single hit to starboard. Rocked by explosions, the gallant *Repulse* capsized and slid beneath the waves in just a matter of minutes.

CONTENTS

THE *RIKKO* CONCEPT

Among the major participants of World War 2, Japan was unique in having its strategic air striking capabilities in the hands of its naval air arm rather than in those of its army (or air force) counterpart. Although it had not begun life in that position, the air service of the Imperial Japanese Navy (IJN) had, by the beginning of the Pacific War, superseded the Imperial Army's air corps as the nation's larger, more modern and more potent air force. This was due, in no small measure, to the Imperial Navy's development in the 1930s of a category of aircraft which it termed *rikujo kogeki-ki* (land-based attack aircraft), commonly referred to in abbreviation as *Rikko*.

During World War 2, naval and marine aviation in other nations, notably the United States, came to operate land-based bomber aircraft in some numbers. However, the majority of these were versions of designs originally produced for the army, and they were used most often in a patrol bomber role, leaving the job of strategic bombardment to their land service brethren. This was not the case in Japan, where it was the navy which eventually took the strategic initiative.

In 1932, Rear Adm Isoroku Yamamoto, Chief of the Technical Division of the Naval Bureau of Aeronautics (*Kaigun Koku Hombu*), launched an ambitious three-year plan aimed at achieving self-sufficiency and technological parity with the West for the navy's air service, and, by extension, the Japanese aviation industry. This plan gave birth to an impressive series of designs which did much to raise Japanese naval aircraft technology to world standards.

Most of these machines were in conventional naval categories, but also among them was a unique new category – the land-based attack aircraft. In IJN terminology, an attack aircraft (*kogeki-ki*) was an aeroplane whose primary mission was attack by aerial torpedo, although it could also carry bombs, while a bomber (*bakugeki-ki*) dropped bombs only.

A standard front view of a Type 1 Land-based Attack Aircraft Model 11 (G4M1) in flight, showing to good advantage the aircraft's rotund, 'cigar-shaped' appearance. Named 'Betty' by Allied Technical Air Intelligence, it was the most widely known Japanese bomber aircraft of World War 2 to friend and foe alike. Note the lack of bomb-bay doors on this aircraft, which was a standard feature on the Type 1 until the advent of later examples of the Model 22. Unlike most bombers, the Type 1 was not fitted with conventional bomb-bay doors which opened and closed, the aircraft's ordnance instead being open to the elements at all times. A wind deflection plate was fitted to the rear of the open bomb-bay to cut down on wind turbulence within the bay. When sortied on a reconnaissance mission, a fairing panel could be fitted over the Type 1's bomb-bay, completely sealing it off (*via Bunrindo K K*)

The brainchild of Vice Adm Shigeru Matsuyama, head of *Koku Hombu*, this aircraft was envisaged as a multi-seat, multi-engined machine capable of attacking warships with torpedoes or bombs far out to sea from land bases, able to support the battle fleet in a decisive naval engagement with the enemy.

Matsuyama issued orders to Yamamoto and his subordinates in the Technical Division to do the necessary research and development work, and their efforts led eventually to the issuance of a 9-*Shi* (1934) prototype specification to Mitsubishi Aircraft Company Ltd. The result was the Type 96 Land-based Attack Aircraft (G3M), officially adopted for service in 1936, and later code-named 'Nell' by the Allies in the Pacific War.

Of all-metal, stressed-skin construction, with retractable landing gear, the 96 *Rikko* at once gave the Imperial Japanese Navy a twin-engined, land-based aircraft fully competitive in performance with the latest bombers in the world. Above all, it possessed the great range necessary to support fleet operations in the vast Pacific Ocean.

The initial production model, the G3M1 Model 11, could carry an 800-kg (1764-lb) payload for 1540 nautical miles (1772 statute miles). In comparison, its near contemporary, the German Heinkel He 111B, could carry nearly twice the bomb load, but for only 565 miles.

In April 1936, shortly after formation of the Kisarazu *Kokutai* (one of the pioneer units of the land attack corps), Capt Takijiro Onishi, head of the Instruction Division at *Koku Hombu*, made an inspection tour of the new unit. Hearing Onishi express his unreserved satisfaction over the new aircraft, Lt Cdr Yoshiharu Soga, Kisarazu *Kokutai's* Air Officer (*Hikocho*), struck a note of caution. 'We cannot afford to remain so pleased with ourselves', he told Onishi. 'With aeroplanes, what's fresh today quickly becomes tomorrow's tired horse. I think we need to start designing the next prototype soon'.

DESIGNING THE SECOND GENERATION

Informal discussions concerning a successor to the Type 96 Land-based Attack Aircraft began in mid-1937, and formal specifications were issued at the end of September that year. These went once again to Mitsubishi on a sole contractor basis, calling for what was termed the (Provisional Designation) 12-*Shi* Land-based Attack Aircraft (G4M1) with the following basic characteristics:

Maximum Speed: 215 knots (247 mph) at 3000 m (9845 ft) altitude
Maximum Range: 2600 nautical miles (2993 miles, or 4815 km)
Range with combat load: 2000 nautical miles (2302 miles, or 3700 km)
Payload: essentially same as Type 96 Land-based Attack Aircraft
Crew: 7 to 9
Powerplant: two 1000 hp X2 (*Kinsei*) engines

These requirements were nothing short of absurd. They demanded a twin-engined machine, powered by the same class of engine used on the G3M1, which would fly 27 knots faster and nothing less than 460 nautical miles farther with the same payload. Beyond a vague desire for better performance, and an almost single-minded pursuit of yet greater range capability, these demands betrayed a lack of clear insight as to how the operational needs of this aircraft category would develop in future. But, undaunted, Mitsubishi took up the challenge.

7

It would be no exaggeration to say that the aircraft which ultimately entered IJN service was the result of brilliant, but strained, engineering by Mitsubishi in order to meet fundamentally unreasonable navy demands.

Kiro Honjo was the natural choice to head the design team. He had been chief designer not only of the 96 *Rikko*, but also of its precursor, the 8-*Shi* Special Reconnaissance Aircraft. He was thus the most experienced aeronautical engineer in Japan at the time in the field of modern bomber design. Following a review of all preliminary data, Honjo concluded that the only sensible way to meet the navy's excessive range demands was to do so with a four-engined design.

At the first planning conference for the new aircraft between the company and the navy, Honjo requested a revision of the specifications, and made a statement strongly urging adoption of a four-engined configuration.

As his initial design proposal, he introduced a four-engined sketch which he had chalked on the blackboard prior to the meeting. At this, Rear Adm Misao Wada, then head of the Technical Division of *Koku Hombu*, and chairman of the conference, retorted in furious temper, 'The navy will decide matters of operational need! Mitsubishi should just keep quiet and build a twin-engined attack aeroplane in accordance with navy specifications. Erase the drawing of the four-engined aeroplane on the blackboard at once!' So ended Honjo's four-engined *Rikko* proposal.

Unknown to Honjo and his colleagues at Mitsubishi, *Koku Hombu* had already unofficially approached the Nakajima Aeroplane Company Ltd during 1937 as the manufacturer of choice for the next land-based attack aircraft following the 12-*Shi* project.

Following his appointment in October 1937 as head of the Technical Division, Wada had arranged for Nakajima to purchase the prototype of the four-engined Douglas DC-4E commercial transport, along with a manufacturing license for this American aircraft. Ostensibly acquired for commercial use by Dai-Nippon Airline Company, the DC-4E was bought to serve as a pattern aircraft for the navy's first four-engined land-based attack aeroplane, eventually to become known as the G5N1 *Shinzan* (Mountain Recess). In the end, however, the *Shinzan* proved a dismal failure.

A major challenge of the 12-*Shi Rikko* project concerned the requirement for a rear-firing 20 mm cannon. This was included in a detailed specification supplement issued to Mitsubishi on 3 December 1937, and was the result of the harsh lessons learned in combat during the undeclared war with China, which had started that summer. The

A formation of Type 96 Land-based Attack Aircraft (G3M2) of the Genzan *Kokutai* are seen in flight sometime in 1940. The 12-*Shi* Land-based Attack Aircraft, which was eventually adopted for service as the Type 1 Land-based Attack Aircraft, was designed as a successor to the 1936-vintage Type 96. Although best known for its service in China from 1937 to 1941, the Type 96 continued to operate alongside the newer Type 1 throughout 1942, and it was not phased out of frontline service until 1943. The large turtle-backed dorsal position housing a 20 mm cannon was a later addition to the original design, and led directly to the installation of a similar weapon in the tail of the Type 1 *Rikko* (via Edward M Young)

This formation of Model 11s of the 1st *Chutai* of the Kanoya *Kokutai* was photographed on a mission over South-east Asia in the early months of the Pacific War. The normal payload for the Model 11 was a single Type 91 aerial torpedo or a combination of ordnance, such as one 800-kg bomb, two 500-kg bombs, four 250-kg bombs or 12 60-kg bombs (*via Robert C Mikesh*)

decision was reached in April 1938 to locate the cannon in a hand-held position in the extreme tail of the 12-*Shi* design.

The adoption of a tail gun position, combined with advances in aerodynamic research, resulted in the new aircraft featuring a rotund, but streamlined fuselage, which reminded many of a cigar, or *hamaki* in Japanese. Honjo and his design team, however, had an altogether less complimentary nickname for their own creation. They called it *namekuji* – the 'slug'.

Confined by the navy's insistence on a twin-engined configuration, the designers faced a serious problem in finding space for the 4900 litres of fuel that had to be crammed into the bomber. Honjo's solution was to use integral fuel tanks. To facilitate this, the main wing was given a double main spar, these combining with chord-wise outer panels to form a torsion box structure within the wing. The space provided by this box was sealed against leakage and used to house fuel cells in which the inner surface of the wing's outer skin itself served as the upper and lower walls of the cells.

A head-on shot of a standard Model 11 on the ground. The flat bombardier's window immediately behind the nose glazing is well illustrated in this view. This feature gave the Type 1 *Rikko* a characteristic 'step' to the profile of the nose undersurface (*Author's Collection*)

As Honjo had previously stressed, this aircraft would be extremely vulnerable to enemy fire. The use of conventional fuel tanks, fully internalised within the airframe, would have left room for the installation of protective measures, but would also have reduced fuel capacity below requirements. The navy, in its collective wisdom, would not accept any shortfall in range or performance, and appeared quite willing to take the risks inherent in the design.

This was mute testimony to the extent to which a tactical doctrine favouring attack at all costs pervaded the Imperial Navy. The IJN was loath to accept the 300-kg weight penalty which the installation of rubber ply protection for the fuel tanks entailed. Ever focused on performance and range in pursuit of the offensive, navy airmen refused to give up that weight in bombs or fuel in exchange for a feature which many still considered nonessential. This view was seemingly vindicated in China, where a combination of higher operating altitude, better formation discipline and, most importantly, the introduction of effective fighter escort dramatically reduced losses over China.

It appeared to the navy that these countermeasures were sufficient to stem prohibitive losses, but the IJN's failure to assess the experience of the air war in China properly would eventually have fatal results for many *Rikko* crews. But all that lay in the future.

One key triumph for Honjo was his decision to replace the 1000-hp *Kinsei* (Venus) engine specified by the navy with a larger, more powerful radial powerplant then under development by Mitsubishi. The navy raised no objection to this change, the new engine (officially named the *Kasei* (Mars) Model 11) successfully passing inspection in September 1938. Rated at 1530 hp for take-off, the 14-cylinder, two row radial *Kasei* gave the design team a realistic chance of meeting the performance requirements which would have been impossible with the older *Kinsei*.

On 23 October 1939, the prototype 12-*Shi* Land-based Attack Aircraft took off on its first test flight from Kagamigahara airfield, north of Nagoya, with Mitsubishi test pilots Katsuzo Shima and Harumi Aratani at the controls. Slight problems in handling qualities and stability were experienced, but, leaving these for resolution in the second prototype, the first machine was accepted by the navy on 24 January 1940.

With an enlarged vertical tail and balancing tabs added to the ailerons, the second prototype began test flights at Kagamigahara on 27 February 1940. Following minor improvements to the rudder, the Mitsubishi test pilots pronounced their complete satisfaction with control and stability, and this machine passed into navy hands on 15 March.

During the course of its test programme, the G4M1 achieved a top speed in excess of 240 knots (276 mph) and a maximum range without payload of 3000 nautical miles (3453 statute miles). Both bettered the specified requirements by some margin, delighting the navy.

'WINGTIP ESCORT'

All seemed ready for the IJN's new land-based attack aircraft to enter production in the spring of 1940, but events in China disrupted new aeroplane's development schedule once again. On 17 May 1940, the navy launched Operation *101*, a four-month assault on the Chinese wartime capital of Chungking and other targets in Szechwan Province, notably

Chengtu, by a concentration of some 130 *Rikko*. These targets lay far beyond the operating radius of the navy's Type 96 Carrier Fighter (A5M), and casualties mounted as the *Rikko* once again endured unescorted missions.

Experience showed that aircraft positioned at the extreme ends of the defensive 'V of V' formations flown by the *Rikko* were most exposed, and duly suffered the highest casualty rates. Taking note of the new 12-*Shi Rikko*'s outstanding performance, the navy wished to modify the basic design into an escort gunship to fly these positions.

Mitsubishi objected strenuously to the escort aeroplane idea, but the navy insisted, and the decision was made to produce 30 of these aeroplanes ahead of the land attack version. Widely referred to as a 'wingtip escort aeroplane', the gunship was officially known as the 12-*Shi Rikujo Kogeki-Ki Kai* (12-*Shi* Land-Based Attack Aircraft Modified) and given the technical short code designation G6M1. Modifications from the basic *Rikko* design included the addition of extra 20 mm cannon and partial protection for the fuel tanks.

The first two G6M1s were completed in August 1940, and as Mitsubishi had warned, the aeroplane failed to meet expectations. General flight characteristics suffered from the additional cannon positions and the resulting rearward travel in its centre of gravity. As the Americans would later learn with their own YB-40 and XB-41 gunship experiments, the Japanese discovered that the overall performance envelope of the G6M1 was simply too far removed from that of the basic *Rikko* design to make joint formation flying of the two models a viable concept.

Ironically, August 1940 saw the operational debut of Mitsubishi's Type 0 Carrier Fighter, or *Rei-sen* (A6M). The Zero, as this superb successor to the Type 96 Carrier Fighter was to become universally known, had the range to fly to practically any remaining target in China. Following its spectacular first combat on 13 September 1940 over Chungking (see *Osprey Aircraft of the Aces 22 - Imperial Japanese Navy Aces 1937-45* for further details), the *Rikkos*' worries were over.

The 'wingtip escort' project delayed service introduction of the G4M1 by almost a year, and underscored the fundamentally flawed approach towards aircraft protection exhibited by the Imperial Navy. With armament removed it was used as a transition trainer for *Rikko* crews, being officially adopted as such in April 1941 as the Type 1 Large Land-based Trainer Model 11 (G6M1-K).

A well-known shot of a Type 1 Land-based Transport Model 11 (G6M1-L) being used as a unit hack by the 3rd *Kokutai*, which, along with the Tainan *Kokutai*, was the main Zero Fighter unit involved in the conquest of South-east Asia. X-902 is painted in the early two-tone green and brown 'China Scheme', and is seen here in the East Indies, probably at Kendari, Celebes, during 1942. Converted from the unsuccessful G6M1 escort gunship, the aircraft lacks the flat bombardier's window panel immediately behind the nose cone glazing, which was a characteristic of the G4M1. And as with all early G4M1s, it has just two rows of windows on the side of the nose. Note also the rear fuselage hatch, which is oval in shape, as opposed to the circular hatch fitted to the standard *rikko* version (*via S Nohara*)

Later still, most of these machines were converted into transports, with seating inside for twenty passengers and a crew of five. Adopted for service in October 1941 as the Type 1 Land-based Transport Model 11 (G6M1-L), they were originally to be used as paratroop carriers, but were flown extensively as squadron hacks and fleet headquarters transports.

SERVICE ACCEPTANCE

At long last, the first production G4M1 was completed in December 1940. Its empty weight had increased to 7000 kg from the first prototype's 6480 kg, but performance was still excellent. The aeroplane could reach a top speed of 231 knots, and could fly 2315 nautical miles in combat overload condition. Its range capabilities greatly exceeded those of foreign contemporary twin-engined bombers, and were more in the league of four-engined 'heavies'. Operational trials conducted by Yokosuka *Kokutai* proceeded smoothly, and the G4M1 was officially adopted for service use on 2 April 1941 as the Type 1 Land-based Attack Aircraft Model 11.

From March 1942 onwards, the G4M1 was fitted with *Kasei* Model 15 engines (larger supercharger than on *Kasei* Model 11), which were first installed on the 241st example (s/n 2241). Officially remaining the Model 11 (often referred to in error as Model 12), the bomber enjoyed better high altitude performance, and *Kasei* 15s were made standard on G4M1s from the 406th aircraft (s/n 2406), built in August 1942. Separate air intakes for carburettors above the engine cowlings were also added on a test model, but not adopted on production aircraft. Externally, *Kasei* 15-powered Model 11 were indistinguishable from those with *Kasei* 11s.

Attempts to give the bomber better protection were initially ineffective, the fire extinguishers and CO_2 chambers behind Nos 1 and 2 fuel tanks proving unable to cope with even modest battle damage. From the 663rd aircraft (s/n 4663, built in March 1943) onwards, 30 mm rubber ply sheet was applied externally to the undersurface of the wings. This reduced the G4M's top speed by five knots and shortened its range by 170 nautical miles. The upper surface of the wings remained unprotected.

Two small 5 mm plates were also fitted behind the tail cannon, their purpose being to protect the gun's 20 mm explosive ammunition, rather than gunner! These also proved useless, failing to stop even 7.7 mm rounds, and they were often removed in the field.

Other modifications included the addition of propeller spinners, the slight lengthening of the engine exhaust stacks and, in the spring of 1943, the cutting away of the outer half of the glazed tail cone in an effort to improve the gunner's field of fire. In August 1943 an entirely redesigned tail cone (with reduced framing and a wide 'V'-shaped cut out) was introduced. Finally, in September 1943 individual engine exhaust stacks were fitted from the 954th machine (s/n 5954) onwards.

Production of the Model 11 ended in January 1944 following the construction of 1170 examples. The aggregate total of the basic design was 1202, this figure including two prototypes and 30 G6M1s.

G4M2

The G4M2 was essentially a Type 1 *Rikko* with *Kasei* Model 21 engines (water-methanol injection, rated at 1850 hp for take-off), the aircraft being provisionally designated the Model 12 – this was subsequently changed to the Model 22. The engines were housed in newly-shaped nacelles with individual exhaust stacks, and they drove four-bladed constant-speed units in place of the three-bladed propellers of the Model 11.

The replacement of the hand-held dorsal 7.7 mm machine gun with a power-operated 20 mm turret was ordered in November 1941, increasing the standard combat weight to 12,500 kg from 9500 kg on G4M1.

The G4M2's wings were also completely redesigned (thicker airfoil and laminar flow), whilst internal fuel capacity was increased to 6490 litres. Again, much of this was housed in integral tanks that were only partly protected by rubber ply on wing undersurfaces. The horizontal tail was strengthened and increased in surface area. To distinguish the numerous changes from the Model 11, Mitsubishi rounded the tips of the main wings, horizontal tail and fin/rudder. The tail wheel was initially made retractable, although this became fixed once again on later models.

The glazed nose cone with its 7.7 mm gun became power-rotated, whilst the area between the nose cone and the front of the cockpit windscreen was extensively glazed, and provision made for two additional 7.7 mm guns to fire from the sides of the nose. Waist gun sponsons were replaced by flat window panels for 7.7 mm, although the tail gun position was the same as on late production Model 11s – a 'V'-shaped cut out. In addition to token armour plates near the tail gun, 10 mm armour plate was fitted inside the dorsal turret.

The G4M2's maiden flight (performed by s/n 2001) took place on 17 December 1942 – three other prototypes were also built. With a maximum range of 3031 nautical miles, this version could fly further than any other G4M. Its maximum speed was 236 knots.

The first production machine (fifth Model 22 s/n 2005) was completed in July 1943, and together with a sixth machine, was retained as a test aircraft because of numerous problems afflicting the revised design. The most serious of these was the vibration of the *Kasei* 21 engines, which was never completely resolved.

According to Mitsubishi documents, the G4M2 was fitted with bulged bomb-bay doors from about the 65th machine onwards, but evidence suggests that these were later removed. From the 105th Model 22 (s/n 2105) built, an optically flat panel was installed on the nose cone glazing as an aid in night bombing.

A close-up of the engine cowling of a late-production Model 11 fitted with individual engine exhaust stacks, which were introduced on the production line from the 954th machine (s/n 5954, in September 1943) onward (*National Archives via S Nohara*)

VARIANTS

The Model 22 *Ko* carried Type 3 *Ku* Mark 6 (H6) search radar, and its fuselage waist 7.7 mm guns were replaced by 20 mm Type 99 Mark 1 cannon. Its side window panels were consequently redesigned and offset, the one to starboard being placed further aft than the one to port.

The Model 22 *Otsu* exchanged its dorsal-turreted 20 mm Type 99 Mark 1 for a longer-barrelled Type 99 Mark 2.

The *Kasei* Model 25 was produced as a result of the change in reduction gear ratio of the *Kasei* Model 21 engine in an effort to solve vibration problems. Flight data obtained on 22 May 1944 with the first aircraft so equipped (s/n 2501) showed a marked improvement in performance, its top speed being 243 knots. The variant was placed in production as the Type 1 Land-based Attack Aircraft Model 24 (G4M2A). In other changes, its engine cowlings were given a separate carburettor air intake on top, and bomb-bay doors were now standard. In all other respects, the aircraft was identical to the Model 22.

Variants of the G4M2A included the Model 24 *Ko*, which carried radar and 20 mm cannon in waist positions just as the Model 22 *Ko* had. The Model 24 *Otsu* exchanged its 20 mm Type 99 Mark 1 in a dorsal turret for the longer-barrelled Type 99 Mark 2, just like the Model 22 *Otsu*. The Model 24 *Hei* swapped its 7.7 mm gun in the nose for a 13 mm Type 2 MG, this weapon being located in the extreme nose tip in place of the radar antenna, which was repositioned above the nose cone.

An early production Model 22 (G4M2) of 762 *Kokutai*, seen at Konoike, Japan, in 1944. The aircraft carries the early short-barrelled Type 99 Mark 1 20 mm cannon in the dorsal turret, and is still equipped with 7.7 mm guns in the nose and waist gun positions. This particular *rikko* was amongst the first 104 Model 22s produced, as is evidenced by the curved nose glazing. A flat panel was incorporated in the nose cone from the 105th machine (s/n 2105) onwards (*via* S Nohara)

This Model 24 *Otsu* (G4M2A) was photographed at Clark Field, in the Philippines, in early 1945. The separate air intake above the engine cowling was characteristic of the Model 24 series. The *Otsu* series also employed a longer-barrelled Type 99 Mark 2 cannon in the dorsal turret, as well as having 20 mm weapons in the waist gun positions. The nose gun remained a 7.7 mm, however (*National Archives via Dana Bell*)

A line up of Model 34 *Otsu* (G4M3A) at Yokosuka following the end of the war. The most noticeable feature of the Model 34 series was the B-17E-like tail gun position and the dihedral on the horizontal tailplanes. The main wing roots were also given small fillets, whilst internally the most important feature was a single-spar wing with fully protected fuel tanks. The aircraft saw only limited service towards the very end of the Pacific War, primarily on transport and maritime patrol duties (*National Archives via S Nohara*)

The Model 24 *Tei* (G4M2E) had its bomb-bay doors removed and fittings installed to carry a MXY 7 *Ohka* (Cherry Blossom) piloted rocket bomb. It also featured armour plate protection for the pilots, fuselage fuel tanks and fuel cocks, as well as a layer of carbon tetra-chloride fluid in No 2 fuel tanks.

The following models were also built, although not in quantity – the Model 25 (G4M2B) was equipped with *Kasei* Model 27 engines, the Model 26 (G4M2C) had *Kasei* Model 25 *Otsu* fuel injection engines and the Model 27 (G4M2D), produced by the Naval Air Technical Arsenal, was equipped with *Kasei* Model 25 *Ru* turbo-supercharged engines.

Some 429 G4M2 and 713 G4M2A (all variants, including derivative models) were produced up until manufacturing ended in June 1945.

G4M3

The G4M3 was the last production model to enter service, boasting protected, internal fuel tanks and a reduced range. The structure of the main wing was redesigned with a single main spar, and small fillets were added to the wing roots. Powered by *Kasei* Model 25 engines, the first prototype (s/n 3001) was flown on New Year's Day 1944. With no rubber pads on wing undersurfaces, the Model 34 attained a maximum speed of 259.7 knots. The 7.7 mm waist guns changed to 20 mm cannon as with the G4M2 series, whilst the tail gun arrangement was completely redesigned along the lines of that fitted to the Boeing B-17E. This shortened the overall length of the fuselage, and caused the aeroplane's centre of gravity to travel forward, affecting stability. This was effectively countered, however, by adding dihedral to the horizontal stabilisers.

Entering production in October 1944 as the Type 1 Land-based Attack Aircraft Model 34 *Ko* (G4M3A), the aircraft's production was greatly hampered by a major earthquake and air raids in the Nagoya area. The total number of Model 34s produced at Nagoya by war's end was estimated to be just 90 machines, whilst the Mitsubishi plant at Misushima, in Okayama Prefecture, had constructed only a solitary example prior to the surrender.

Variants produced included the Model 34 *Otsu*, which was modified in an identical way to the previously-mentioned Model 22 *Otsu* and Model 24 *Otsu*. The Model 34 *Hei* was also built, equipped in a similar fashion to the Model 24 *Hei*. Finally, the Model 37 was a Mitsubishi design fitted with turbo-supercharged engines.

Total production of all Type 1 *Rikko* models was estimated to be 2435.

INTO SERVICE

By the beginning of 1941 there were six *Kokutai* of land-based attack aircraft in the air service of the Imperial Japanese Navy. All were *josetsu* (standard establishment) *Kokutai*, designated by the name of their home bases and forming part of the standing peacetime force structure.

The Kisarazu and Kanoya *Kokutai* were the oldest. They had taken the Type 96 Land-based Attack Aircraft into combat for the first time in August 1937 and boasted proud histories. Partially since 1938, and totally from January 1940, Kisarazu *Kokutai* had functioned as a training unit for *Rikko* crews at its home base on the eastern shores of Tokyo Bay.

With its long runways, Kisarazu was ideal for the operation of large aircraft, and it held a special place in the hearts of all *Rikko* crews as the cradle of their corps. The Kanoya *Kokutai*, meanwhile, remained on frontline duty at its base on the southern Japanese island of Kyushu.

Further south still, the Takao *Kokutai* was based at Takao (Kao-hsiung) on the island of Taiwan, which had been a part of the Japanese Empire since 1895. The Chitose *Kokutai* guarded the north from its base on Hokkaido. Two new *Rikko* units had been formed in late 1940, the Mihoro *Kokutai* in northern Hokkaido and the Genzan *Kokutai* at Genzan (Wonsan) in Korea, also a part of the Japanese Empire since its annexation in 1910.

In order to concentrate the navy's growing land-based air power under a single, strategic command, the 11th Air Fleet (*Koku Kantai*) was formed on 15 January 1941, bringing under its direct control all of the frontline *Rikko* units of the Imperial Japanese Navy. On 10 April 1941 two additional *Kokutai* – the 1st and 3rd – joined the ranks of the navy's *Rikko* force. These were *tokusetsu* (special establishment) *Kokutai*, given numerical designations and formed for specific field operations on a temporary basis. The 1st *Kokutai* formed at Kanoya, and the 3rd *Kokutai* at Takao.

The *kokutai*, often abbreviated as *Ku*, was the main tactical organisation of the Imperial Navy's air service. Composed of a *hikokitai* (literally an aircraft echelon, but usually referred to in shortened form as *hikotai*, or flying echelon) with its aircraft and aircrews, as well as various ground echelons which provided aircraft maintenance and air base service functions, the *kokutai* was a large, fully integrated organisation.

All personnel in a *kokutai* were organised into 'squads' called *buntai*. Within the *hikotai*, each *buntai* was made up of the requisite number of men necessary to fly and maintain one *chutai* of aircraft. The number of men in a *buntai* would therefore vary depending on the mission role of the unit, and the type of aircraft operated.

Navy airmen tended to use the terms *buntai* and *chutai* interchangeably, but strictly speaking, *buntai* referred to the personnel, while *chutai* referred to the aircraft or the tactical formation in the air. Thus, the *buntaicho* (*buntai* leader) on the ground would be the *chutaicho* in flight. For *rikko* units a standard *chutai* was composed of nine aircraft, plus three in reserve.

The smallest tactical formation was a *shotai* of three aircraft. The number of *chutai* in a *hikotai* would vary, but generally ranged between three and six. The senior officer in a *hikotai* (the most high-ranking to lead in the air under normal circumstances) was the *hikotaicho*, usually a lieutenant commander. Above him was the air officer or *hikocho*, usually a commander. The *hikocho* often doubled as executive officer, second in command to the *kokutai* CO, who usually held the rank of captain.

In May 1941 the Takao *Kokutai*, considered the most highly trained at the time, became the first to convert to the new Type 1 Land-based Attack Aircraft. Next to receive the aircraft was the Kisarazu *Kokutai*, with several being delivered during July and August for training purposes. This allowed the unit to begin turning out crews familiar with the G4M.

COMBAT DEBUT

Operation *101* in 1940 had taught the Japanese that the collective will of civilian populations to withstand aerial assault was a mighty durable thing. Although Japanese aeroplanes ruled the sky over China, the government of Chiang Kai-shek showed no inclination to sue for peace.

In July 1941, the Japanese launched Operation *102*. Most of the land attack aeroplanes of the 11th Air Fleet – some 180 *rikko* – were placed temporarily under the control of the China Area Fleet and flown into bases around Hankow for another round of intensive raids on targets in Szechwan, concentrating once more on Chungking and Chengtu.

By this stage relations between Japan and the United States were deteriorating rapidly, and the Japanese were determined to keep the Chinese beaten down while they still had excess forces available for the task.

As part of this deployment, the Takao *Kokutai* flew into Hankow on 25 July with 30 of their new Type 1 Land Attack Aeroplanes (27 plus three reserves). Two days later they took part in their first combat mission when Operation *102* commenced with a raid on Chengtu, but the Chinese offered no aerial resistance on this occasion.

Following the *Rei-sen*'s first appearance over China the previous summer, and the devastation it had caused amongst its foes in the air, the Chinese had deliberately avoided combat with the new fighter. The air war had now become a game of cat and mouse, with the Japanese trying to devise stratagems for catching the Chinese, who did their best to remain elusive. Only when they were sure of meeting unescorted bombers would the Chinese fighters stand and fight.

The Japanese were certain that if the Zeros could fly towards enemy airfields just before dawn, they would be unobserved by lookouts or mistaken for bombers, and would catch the Chinese on the ground at daybreak. But no matter how skilled the fighter pilots were, they could not navigate and fly formation at night over the long distances involved on their own. The arrival of the Type 1 *Rikko* appeared to offer a solution.

The 170-knot cruising speed of the Type 1 was nearly as fast as that of the Zero, allowing both aircraft to hold steady formation with each other, something which the Zero could not do with the slower 96 *Rikko*. A scheme was hatched whereby the Type 1s of *Takao Ku* would act as navigational motherships for the Zeros in the dark.

Within the larger context of Operation *102*, this plan was designated Operation *O-go*, and carried out on 11 August. On the preceding day,

20 *Rei-sen* of the 12th *Kokutai* flew into Ichang, the forward staging base closest to Chinese lines. Nine Type 1 *Rikko* of Takao *Ku* under the command of Lt Yogoro Seto departed Hankow at 0135 on the 11th and headed for Ichang. As the land attack aeroplanes flew almost directly overhead in single file, the fighters took off in the dark and formed up with the *rikko* column. Two *rikko* and four fighters then veered off on diversionary raids to Hanzhong and Guangyuan, but the rest headed for Chengtu, arriving there at 0505.

The Chinese had received warning of approaching Japanese aircraft just in time for Tupolev SB-2 (or possibly SB-3s) bombers of the 1st and 2nd *Da Dui* (Group) to clear their base at Wen Chang before the Zeros arrived. But sure enough, only expecting to meet bombers, the Chinese scrambled Polikarpov I-153 biplane fighters of the 4th *Da Dui* from their base at Shuang Liu.

Six interceptors took off before the Zeros came down to strafe at 0530, the last four aeroplanes of 4th *Da Dui* being caught on the ground. At Wen Chang they destroyed two Tupolev bombers which had been unable to take off, and in the air the Type 1 *Rikko* and the Zeros between them claimed five I-153s shot down. Chinese records indicate two pilots were killed outright, a third one wounded in action later died of injuries sustained in a crash-landing and a fourth crashed while trying to land his mechanically defective fighter. The Japanese suffered no casualties.

The Type 1 *Rikko*, acting only as navigational guides for the Zeros, dropped no bombs on this occasion. What was noteworthy about Operation *O-go* was the extraordinary level of flying skill displayed by the IJN airmen, particularly the fighter pilots. The distance from Ichang to Chengtu was longer than the average distance from British air bases to Hamburg, and flying that far in a single-seat fighter in formation at night, and then returning the same distance after combat over the target, was an incredible feat in 1941.

For the twin-engined *rikko*, flying directly from Hankow, the mission was 47 miles farther than from London to Berlin – a cogent reminder that, in matters of distance, the air war in Asia was of a different order of magnitude from the one in Europe.

Operation *102* was originally planned to last three months, but the situation in the Far East outside China was quickly approaching flash point. In July 1941, Japanese forces moved into southern French Indochina, and the United States countered by freezing all Japanese assets in the US, and together with the Dutch and the British Commonwealth, cut off all supplies of foreign oil.

Although designed to deter the Japanese from further expansion, this action spurred them instead into detailed planning for the capture of the oil and mineral resources of the Dutch East Indies through force of arms before their stores of vital raw materials ran out. Opera-

These Kanoya *Kokutai* Type 1 *Rikko* were photographed during a torpedo attack training exercise held in October 1941 off the Japanese coast. At the start of the Pacific War, Kanoya *Ku* was considered the most highly trained *rikko* unit in the torpedo bomber role (*via S Nohara*)

tion *102* was prematurely terminated on 31 August, and the *rikko* units in the Hankow area all returned to their home bases on 1 and 2 September. With the exception of a small coastal presence, the Imperial Navy's air arm now withdrew completely from China, leaving it in the hands of the Japanese Army Air Force. Navy airmen now began a programme of the most intense training in preparation for war with the West.

GATHERING STORM

Following its return to Kanoya from Hankow on 2 September, the Kanoya *Kokutai* became the second combat unit to convert to the Type 1 Land-based Attack Aircraft. At the same time the 3rd *Kokutai* became a fighter organisation equipped with *Rei-sen*. The unit relinquished its Type 96 Land Attack Aeroplanes, and its four *buntai* of *rikko* flight personnel were divided between the Takao and Kanoya *Kokutai*, swelling the ranks of these Type 1 *rikko* units into organisations of six *chutai* each.

The pace of war preparation rose in October. With the big carriers of the 1st Air Fleet committed to a pre-emptive strike against the US Pacific Fleet at Pearl Harbor, the task of providing naval air support for Japan's main southward thrust lay with the land-based units of 11th Air Fleet. As in China, the limited range of the army's bombers dictated that the long-ranging *rikko* of the IJN would shoulder the main burden of strikes deep inside enemy territory.

From their bases on Taiwan, the 21st and 23rd *Koku Sentai* (Air Flotillas) would attack American airpower in the Philippines and provide the strategic element in that air campaign. From bases in southern French Indochina, the 22nd *Koku Sentai* would support the army's drive down the Malay Peninsula to Singapore, Britain's bastion in the Far East.

The original plans for the Philippine campaign had called for the fighters to operate from light carriers positioned off the Philippine coast. However, using their experience in China to advantage, the Zero pilots demonstrated that they could fly the 500-nautical mile distance to Manila and back directly from their bases on southern Taiwan. The carriers were released for other duties, and the pilots of the 3rd and Tainan *Ku* prepared to fly the longest fighter escort missions ever attempted.

Missions of comparable length with single-engined fighters would not take place in Europe until the spring of 1944 when P-51Bs began escorting US Eighth Air Force bombers all the way to Berlin and back.

Another Kanoya machine makes a practice run on the IJN battleship *Nagato*, which served as flagship of the Combined Fleet until the 'superbattleship' *Yamato* took over in 1942. These training exercises, staged in October and November 1941, paid off handsomely the following month when the main body of Kanoya *Ku* was instrumental in sinking the British battleship HMS *Prince of Wales* and the battlecruiser HMS *Repulse* off Malaya on 10 December (*via S Nohara*)

But one problem remained. The timing of the attack on Pearl Harbor, coupled with the difference in time zones over the vast area in which the Japanese intended to open hostilities, implied that American forces in the Philippines would be fully alerted by the time the Japanese struck.

Attack at dawn was imperative, but having rejected the option of launching their fighters from carrier decks near the Philippine coast, the only solution lay in a five-hour mass formation flight from Taiwan in the dead of night. Operation *O-go* in August had set an invaluable precedent, and the aircrews of the Type 1 *Rikko* and the *Rei-sen* pilots now trained to repeat that performance, but on a scale and over a distance of hitherto unimagined proportions.

On 31 October the 24th *Koku Sentai*, with the Chitose *Kokutai* under its command, left 11th Air Fleet control and came under 4th Fleet, which had the task of capturing the American islands of Guam and Wake in the Central Pacific when hostilities opened. The Type 96 Land Attack Aeroplanes of Chitose *Ku* had already completed their deployment to the Japanese-mandated Marshall Islands during the second half of October. In mid-November, a single Type 1 *Rikko* was assigned to the Chitose *Ku* and flown out to Roi, in Kwajalein Atoll, by Lt Nobuo Ando.

By now the feeling that war would soon come to the Far East was universal. On 25 October the British had despatched their newest battleship, HMS *Prince of Wales*, from home waters, bound for the Orient, and by 4 November the Americans had six B-17C and twenty-nine B-17D Flying Fortresses at Clark Field, on Luzon, their major air base in the Philippines. More were expected in December.

On 18 November the 1st *Kokutai* moved to Tainan, on the island of Taiwan, and four days later the Kanoya *Kokutai* deployed to nearby Taichu (Tai-chung). By this time the 22nd *Koku Sentai* HQ was at Saigon, in French Indochina, while its subordinate units, the Genzan and Mihoro *Kokutai*, completed their deployment there by month's end.

On 30 November Kanoya *Ku* was suddenly alerted to transfer half its strength to Saigon. Forty-eight hours earlier HMS *Prince of Wales* had reached Colombo, Ceylon, and then, in company with the battlecruiser *Repulse*, which had preceded her there, had sailed for Singapore. The transport *Keiyo Maru* was loaded in Takao Harbour with aviation fuel, Type 91 *Kai* 2 aerial torpedoes and other vital stores for Kanoya *Ku*, then despatched to Indochina. The transfer of the air echelon would take place later, timed to coincide with the transport's arrival.

On 2 December – the day the *Prince of Wales* and *Repulse* arrived at Singapore amid great fanfare – the Kanoya *Ku* air echelon was ordered to move. Choosing the units he felt were most proficient in torpedo attack, the *kokutai* commander, Capt Naoshiro Fujiyoshi, led the 36 Type 1 *Rikko* (27 plus nine reserves) of the 1st, 2nd and 3rd *Chutai* to Saigon.

Hampered by stormy weather over the South China Sea on their initial attempts, the *kokutai* successfully completed its transfer on 5 December. Two days later it moved to Thu Dau Moi, which was a new base 20 km north-east of Saigon. With the *kokutai* CO leading, this half of the unit officially became the main body, with the 4th, 5th, and 6th *Chutai* remaining on Taiwan (led by *Hikocho* Lt Cdr Toshiie Irisa) becoming the detachment.

On the eve of the Pacific War the 11th Air Fleet had 216 *rikko*

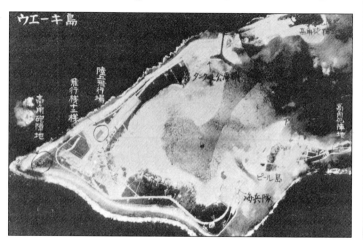

This reconnaissance photograph of Wake Island was taken during a clandestine pre-war mission flown on 4 December 1941 by the Chitose *Kokutai's* Lt Nobuo Ando in the unit's sole Type 1 *Rikko*. North is towards the bottom of this view, which has been reversed for captioning by the Japanese photo interpreters. Thus, Peacock Point is at the left end of this shot. The middle of the three vertical notations along the left side of the photograph indicates 'twelve aircraft', referring to the dozen F4F-3 Wildcats of VMF-211 which had just arrived on Wake that very morning (*via Edward M Young*)

One of the most historic strike photographs of the Pacific War captures the attack on Clark Field, in the Philippines, shortly after noon on 8 December 1941. The two clusters of bomb bursts from Type 1 *Rikko* of Takao *Kokutai* and Type 96 *Rikko* of 1st *Kokutai* form a tight pattern across the centre of the field and hangar facilities. The neat rows of barracks at Fort Stotsenberg may be seen at the top of the picture (*Author's Collection*)

(excluding reserve aircraft) on strength. Half of these were the Type 1 Land-based Attack Aircraft of the Takao and Kanoya *Kokutai* with 54 each. The rest were the older Type 96 machines of the 1st, Genzan and Mihoro *Kokutai*, each with 36 aeroplanes. Separately, the Chitose *Kokutai* had 27 Type 96 and a lone Type 1 *Rikko* at Roi, in the Marshall Islands.

THE STORM BREAKS

Sunday, 7 December 1941 is seared in American memory as the day the Pacific War began quite simply because Pearl Harbor lies to the east of the International Dateline. For Japan and the rest of Asia, as well as the American island possessions of Guam and Wake, lying to the west of that imaginary line in the mid Pacific, the war began on Monday, 8 December.

The final decision to go to war had been taken by Japan on 1 December. Next day, the historic message 'Climb Mount Niitaka 1208' had gone out to all IJN forces, setting the fateful day.

On 4 December, the sole Type 1 *Rikko* of Chitose *Ku* took off from Roi with Lt Nobuo Ando in command and headed for Wake Island, 590 nautical miles to the north. Flying over at almost 9000 metres' altitude, he managed to obtain a clear, panoramic photograph of the entire atoll. Captured on film were Wake's defences, including 12 Grumman F4F-3s of VMF-211, which had just arrived that morning aboard the carrier USS *Enterprise* (see *Osprey Aircraft of the Aces 3 - Wildcat Aces of World War 2* for further details).

From Taiwan, similar missions were flown over the Philippines during the final week of peace. The last full dress rehearsal involving pre-dawn take-offs of fighters and *rikko* was conducted on 5 December, and thereafter, all personnel were confined to base. As prearranged, the Kanoya *Kokutai* Detachment moved down from Taichu to Takao on the 7th. That evening, each *Kokutai* commander announced to his men the opening of hostilities against the United States, the British Common-wealth and the Netherlands East Indies.

Sunrise at Manila on 8 December would be at 0609 local time. Plans called for the land attack aeroplanes and fighters of the 11th Air Fleet to take off from their bases on Taiwan commencing at 0130, and after a time-consuming assembly in the dark, followed by a fuel-conserving slow cruise, hit their targets shortly after dawn at 0630. Some 27 Type 1 *Rikko* of Takao *Kokutai* and 27 more from Kanoya *Ku*, escorted by 54 *Rei-sen* from 3rd and Tainan *Ku*, would hit Nichols Field, the main American fighter base on the outskirts of Manila. A further 27 Type 1 *Rikko* of Takao *Ku*, along with 27 Type 96 *Rikko* of 1st *Ku*, escorted by 36 *Rei-sen* from Tainan *Ku*, had the main bomber base of Clark Field as their target, the latter being situated some 50 nautical miles closer to Taiwan.

At about 2230 on 7 December, fog began to build up in the Tainan area. Overnight fog over southern Taiwan was common around this time of year, but normally did not linger. That night, however, proved exceptional, and by midnight it had become a thick milky soup, and showed no sign of clearing. A half-hour later it had spread to the Takao area as well.

At 0100 on 8 December Vice Adm Nishiso Tsukahara, C-in-C 11th Air Fleet, called a meeting of subordinate commanders. American radio messages intercepted earlier were interpreted to mean that US pursuit forces had deployed north from the Manila area to a defence line running through Iba and Clark. This, together with the fog-induced delay in take off, caused Tsukahara to abandon the opening day's strike on the Manila area. The mission to Clark Field remained unchanged, but for the units selected to attack Nichols Field, a last minute change of target now took place – 54 Type 1 *Rikko* prepared instead to deal a sledgehammer blow against the tiny airfield at Iba.

The fog at Tainan finally began to lift at 0750, and the slow Type 96 Land Attackers of the 1st *Kokutai* took off at 0815. One crashed on take off, leaving 26 to carry out the mission. The Zeros at Tainan followed an hour later. At Takao, the fog finally lifted around 0900, just in time for the rescheduled take off. Starting at 0930, the 54 Type 1s of Takao *Ku* and the 27 of Kanoya *Ku* roared down the runway, followed by the Zeros.

Mount Niitaka, the highest peak on Taiwan, could be seen clearly in the distance as the aeroplanes formed up. In the full light of morning there was no need to execute the well rehearsed night formation flights, but any worries over mid-air collisions in the dark were replaced by yet graver concerns. The attack on Pearl Harbor had been followed by early morning raids directly on the Philippines, with Davao, on the southern island of Mindanao, being hit by aeroplanes from the carrier *Ryujo*.

Targets in northern Luzon had also been attacked by Japanese army bombers, which had taken off according to their original schedule, unhampered by fog at their bases in the extreme south of Taiwan. With so much prior warning, US fighters would surely be up in full force.

Half of Takao *Ku* (led by the *hikocho*, Cdr Yoshiso Suda, flying as observer in the lead Type 1 piloted by Lt Jiro Adachi) and the 26 *rikko* of Kanoya *Ku*, one having aborted (led by their *hikocho*, Lt Cdr Irisa), headed for Iba. The other half of Takao *Ku* (led by the *hikotaicho*, Lt Cdr Taro Nonaka), together with the Type 96s of 1st *Ku*, with which they caught up en route, made for Clark Field. The land attackers went in high at 7000 metres, fully expecting to have to fight their way into the target. For them, what followed was thoroughly anticlimactic.

As is well known, American fighters had been up since the morning, waiting for an early attack. But, unaware of the weather problems on Taiwan, and with the Japanese conspicuously absent over any major targets during these hours, most had landed to refuel when the *rikkos* arrived.

At Clark, the mixed force of Type 1 and Type 96 *Rikko* dropped 636 60-kg bombs – a little over 42 tons – at 1236. The pattern was perfect.

Not a single bomb strayed more than 60 metres outside the perimeter of the field, and the bombing and subsequent strafing by the Zeros destroyed 12 B-17s and damaged five others. A further 20 P-40Bs and several miscellaneous aircraft were also written off as a result of the attack.

Iba was hit by 486 60-kg and 26 250-kg bombs a few minutes after Clark. Seven P-40Es were destroyed on the ground there, and although the Japanese were unaware of it, the only operational radar set in the Philippines was also wrecked. The Americans also lost six other fighters shot down during the course of the day, and at a stroke, half of its heavy bomber force and over 35 per cent of its pursuit strength in the Philippines had been wiped out. In exchange, the Japanese had had just seven Zeros shot down, whilst a Type 1 *Rikko* of Kanoya *Ku* crash-landed short of its base during the return flight.

THE HUNT FOR *FORCE Z*

In the pre-dawn hours of 8 December, the Type 96 Land Attackers of 22nd *Koku Sentai* struggled through severe weather to deliver the war's first bombs on Singapore. The Type 1 *Rikko* of the Kanoya *Kokutai* Main Body, however, remained on the ground. Assigned the specific task of dealing with the British Eastern Fleet, centred around the battleship HMS *Prince of Wales* and the battlecruiser *Repulse*, they waited in readiness for their chance to strike.

A Type 98 Land-based Reconnaissance Aircraft (C5M2 'Babs') reported the two capital ships in port on the 8th. They were still there at 0950 the following morning according to another reconnaissance flight, so preparations were begun to bomb the ships in port that night before they slipped out to sea. Then at 1540 came an unexpected report from submarine I-65, which claimed to have sighted two '*Repulse* Class battleships' (sic) in the South China Sea at 1345. The contact report was almost two hours old.

A hurried re-examination of the reconnaissance photograph taken over Singapore that morning now revealed that the aeroplane's crew had mistaken two large tankers for the 'battlewagons'. The resulting message to all units confirming that the British warships had broken out galvanised Japanese naval forces in the area.

HMS *Prince of Wales* departs Seletar Naval Base, Singapore, on the afternoon of 8 December 1941 on her last operation. Two days later, the mighty battleship was at the bottom of the South China Sea, sunk by aerial attack from the Type 1 *Rikko* of the Kanoya and Type 96 *Rikko* of the Genzan and Mihoro *Kokutai*
(*Imperial War Museum*)

Rear Adm Sir Tom Phillips, C-in-C British Eastern Fleet, had departed Seletar Naval Base, Singapore, at 1735 on 8 December aboard his flagship, *Prince of Wales*, together with the *Repulse* and four destroyers. Collectively known as *Force Z*, the ships had sailed north to attack the concentration of Japanese transports supporting the landing at Singora, in southern Thailand.

Upon learning of the sortie by the British ships, Vice Adm Jisaburo Ozawa, C-in-C Southern Expeditionary Fleet, ordered that a search and attack mission be carried out by the *Rikko* units in the Saigon area. However, this attempt to hunt down *Force Z* on the 9th was thwarted by deteriorating weather and the gathering darkness.

When he recalled his search aeroplanes and cancelled the night attack, Rear Adm Matsunaga, commander of the 22nd *Koku Sentai*, decided on an all-out search and attack mission for the following day. While the Type 96s of the Genzan and Mihoro *Kokutai* would go out with a mixture of bombs and torpedoes, the Type 1 *Rikko* of Kanoya *Ku* would sortie as an all torpedo-armed force.

At 0644 the three *Chutai* of Kanoya *Ku* Main Body began taking off from Thu Dau Moi. They carried Type 91 *Kai* 2 torpedoes, designed for running in shallow depth, and with more powerful warheads than the Type 91 *Kai* 1 torpedoes carried by the Type 96 *Rikko*.

The weather had improved greatly from the evening before, although scattered clouds were evident as the aeroplanes flew south. Meanwhile, Adm Phillips had abandoned his raid on Singora after his vessels were spotted the day before by Japanese cruiser floatplanes, *Force Z* instead now heading back to Singapore. A little after 1000, a Genzan *Rikko* flying the 3rd search sector finally found the British ships, and at 1015 it signalled, 'Enemy main force sighted. North Latitude 4 degrees, East Longitude 103 degrees 55 minutes. Bearing 60 degrees'.

Receiving this signal at Saigon, 22nd *Koku Sentai* immediately relayed the message to all units then in the air.

The aircraft of Genzan and Mihoro *Ku* all heard the first sighting report and headed immediately towards *Force Z*, but the men of Kanoya *Ku*, having flown farther south in their faster Type 1 *Rikko*, did not. By 1028

HMS *Repulse* follows *Prince of Wales* out through the Straits of Johore towards the open sea on 8 December 1941. Despite putting up a brave fight, the battlecruiser ultimately succumbed to the Type 91 *Kai* 2 torpedoes of the Kanoya *Kokutai* some 48 hours after this photograph was taken (*Imperial War Museum*)

they were 600 nautical miles from base, and could see Singapore 80 miles to their right and the coast of Sumatra up ahead – but not *Force Z*. Reluctantly, they turned and headed back north.

On the ground at Thu Dau Moi, the unit's CO, Capt Fujiyoshi, was worried and anxious that his men had not heard the contact report. He telephoned 22nd *Koku Sentai* HQ and requested that the enemy's position be sent in the clear, and Adm Matsunaga obliged by transmitting the enemy's position in plain language at 1130. Kanoya *Ku* caught this signal as they flew north-west of the Anambas Islands, and finally turned on a heading towards *Force Z*.

Hikotaicho Lt Cdr Shichiso Miyauchi led the entire formation of 26, sitting as observer in the lead aeroplane piloted by 1st *Chutai* Leader, Lt Miyoshi Nabeta. Following to the left of the lead *chutai's* nine aircraft were the eight *rikkos* of Lt Moritaka Higashi's 2nd *Chutai*, while the nine aeroplanes of Lt Haruki Iki's 3rd *Chutai* flew their customary position on the lead *chutai's* right.

A layer of cloud beneath the Kanoya formation hid the ocean below as they reached, then passed, *Force Z's* reported position. Then, through a break in the clouds, Miyauchi caught a fleeting glimpse of what looked like a seaplane down below. It was, in fact, a Walrus amphibian catapulted off HMS *Repulse*.

Sensing that they were close to the enemy warships, Miyauchi led the Kanoya formation down through the clouds, with the two following *Chutai* now trailing in line astern. At 1215 the aeroplanes broke through the cloud ceiling at 800 metres altitude, heading north. Then, as they approached the edge of the cloud bank two minutes later, they saw the enemy ships.

About 11 nautical miles ahead and 60 degrees to their right, on a south-easterly course, steamed *Prince of Wales*. The *Repulse* trailed 2500 metres behind and to starboard of the flagship in quarter-line formation, with three destroyers in the van, 2000 metres ahead of the 'Prince'.

When Kanoya *Ku* found their quarry the ships had already sustained damage from earlier attacks by the Type 96 Land Attackers of Mihoro and Genzan *Ku*. Between 1115 and 1157, a total of 32 Type 96s had attacked *Force Z* in successive waves, *Repulse* being hit amidships by a 250-kg bomb from the first high level attack by Mihoro *Ku*. The resulting damage, however, had done nothing to impair her fighting abilities. Through brilliant handling of his ship, Capt W G Tennant managed to comb all 15 torpedoes subsequently launched against *Repulse* by elements from both *Kokutai*.

Prince of Wales, on the other hand, was not so fortunate. A low-level assault by Genzan *Ku* had put two torpedoes into the after portion of the ship on the port side, crippling the rudder and jamming the port propeller shafts. Half the ship's machinery had been destroyed, depriving the battleship of her ability to steer and to fire her after heavy anti-aircraft guns. She had managed to shoot down one of her attackers, but had immediately taken on a 13-degree list to port and had lost ten knots of speed. Although in no immediate danger of sinking, *Prince of Wales* was now a sitting duck for Kanoya *Ku*.

At first the low cloud bank, dropping to 300 metres in places, obscured the approach of the Kanoya formation from the British. However, by the time the nine aeroplanes of Miyauchi's lead *Chutai* had closed the distance to eight miles, the clouds had suddenly lifted to reveal bright blue sky. At the same instant came a barrage of anti-aircraft fire from all five ships of *Force Z*. Miyauchi rocked his wings twice, signalling the attack. It was 1218.

As Miyauchi led the 1st *Chutai* against the starboard side of the *Prince of Wales*, *Repulse* cranked up to 28 knots and began a turn to starboard, presenting her bow to the oncoming aeroplanes. Unaware that *Prince of Wales* had lost her steering, the second and third *shotai* leaders in Miyauchi's *Chutai* assumed that the vessel would do the same and began to turn left in anticipation of such a manoeuvre. But the 'Prince' continued to plough straight ahead, forcing the six aeroplanes to quickly switch targets to *Repulse*.

Miyauchi's lead *shotai* of three aircraft had continued straight on their course, and were now set up beautifully against a large target which took no evasive action and was running at reduced speed. As they closed the distance to the battleship, Nabeta's co-pilot, FPO1/c Danjo reached for the release handle, but Miyauchi stayed his hand. 'Not yet', he ordered.

It was standard procedure during training to release the torpedo at 1000 metres from the target, but Miyauchi was determined to bore into half that distance to insure a hit. At 500 metres he and the No 3 aeroplane of the lead *shotai* dropped their torpedoes, and they saw both hit the ship at 1220 – one near the bow and another just forward of the bridge. At the last moment the view from the No 2 aeroplane was blocked by a close anti-aircraft barrage, causing the crew to miss their chance to fire. The pilot, Flight Seaman Tsutsumi, hurdled over the ship and came around to release from the port side, but failed to score a hit.

Meanwhile, the six aeroplanes of the second and third *shotai* were racing neck and neck with *Repulse*, the battlecruiser straining to tighten its turn as the *rikko* banked sharply to catch her broadside. The aeroplanes won the race and caught the ship from both sides, two attacking to starboard and three to port. *Repulse* finally took a torpedo on the port side near the aft funnel, but continued to steam at 25 knots.

During the attack run, the aircraft of the 3rd *Shotaicho*, FCPO Tokiyoshi Nishikawa, was set afire by AA, but the flames were extinguished and he stayed in the air. The No 2 aeroplane in his *shotai*, unable to gain a good launch position against the battlecruiser, switched back to *Prince of Wales* and put a third torpedo into the battleship's starboard side.

Hard on the heels of the lead *chutai* came the eight aeroplanes of Lt Higashi's 2nd *Chutai*, the six *rikkos* of its first and second *shotai* going after *Repulse* from her port side. The two-aeroplane third *shotai* aimed for her starboard side, but being unable to turn sharply enough to gain a good attack angle there, veered away and attacked *Prince of Wales* to starboard. One of their torpedoes – the fourth to hit the flagship on the starboard side – damaged the outer propeller shaft and gave the *coup de grace* to the vessel. *Repulse*, however, still had a lot of fight left in her. She managed to comb the six torpedoes aimed at her by the first and second *shotai* and nearly brought down Lt Higashi;

'We felt a big shock, then I noticed that one-and-a-half metres of our outer left wing had been blown away. The aileron was buffeting like crazy and looked like it would tear off at any minute. I thought maybe this was the end, but we managed to keep flying just above the waves.'

Last on the scene were the nine aeroplanes of Lt Haruki Iki's 3rd *Chutai*. Iki's task was to size up the situation as he brought up the rear, and add the weight of his *Chutai's* attack where it was most needed. Seeing water spouts rise in succession from *Prince of Wales*, he decided to give *Repulse* his *Chutai's* undivided attention.

By now the battlecruiser had completed a full circle, and Iki led his *shotai* in an attack from the port side. Simultaneously, the six other aeroplanes of his *Chutai* closed on *Repulse* from its starboard side, both formations encountering furious anti-aircraft fire from the ship. Iki released his torpedo some 800 metres from the ship, at a height of 30 metres.

With his payload gone, he firewalled the throttles and leaped over the battlecruiser, almost scraping her bridge. As he did so Iki glanced back to see his No 2, commanded by FPO1/c Fukumatsu Yamamoto, erupt in a ball of orange red flame and go down 300 metres short of the ship's port side. In the next instant, the No 3 *rikko*, commanded by FPO1/c Yuso Nakajima, suffered the same fate. Both wingmen had, however, launched their torpedoes before they went down, and their aim was true. So was Iki's.

Three huge columns of water shot into the air from the port side of *Repulse* – one near the engine room, one by the aft main turret and one by the stern. The six aeroplanes which attacked from the starboard side also gained one hit, alongside 'E' boiler room. The gallant battlecruiser was doomed, and her end came quickly. Two minutes after Capt Tennant ordered abandon ship, HMS *Repulse* capsized and sank stern first at 1233.

Prince of Wales lingered for almost an hour more, but what followed after Kanoya *Kokutai's* attack was mere anticlimax. Two *chutai* of high level Type 96s from Mihoro *Ku* dropped 500-kg bombs and scored one hit amidships at 1243, but the battleship was already finished. Ten minutes after the order to abandon ship was given, the vessel also capsized and went under at 1320. Among the drowned were Adm Phillips and the ship's captain, J C Leach.

There was jubilation among the *rikko* crews. Not only had they won a tremendous victory and removed the greatest obstacle to the army's drive on Singapore, but, for the first time in aviation history, aircraft alone had destroyed capital ships in full combat manoeuvre at sea. In so doing, the *rikko* crews had vindicated the assertions of naval air advocates everywhere, demonstrating the primacy of the aeroplane over the battleship in the most dramatic fashion.

Lt Iki's two wingmen and a Genzan *Ku* Type 96 were the only direct losses for the Japanese, although FCPO Nishikawa's badly damaged aircraft bellied in among rice paddies south-west of Soc Trang when it ran out of fuel. The crew escaped unharmed, however. Three other Type 1 *Rikko* and one Type 96 from Mihoro *Ku* required depot repair.

When Haruki Iki next flew over the scene of battle, on 18 December, he cast two bouquets of flowers onto the waves. He did so, he said, in memory both of his fallen wingmen and of the two great ships and their crew. At least one man had room in his heart for an act of chivalry in the opening days of this new war which, very quickly, would come to be fought with utmost savagery.

ON THE CUTTING EDGE

The drive to acquire the natural resources of the Netherlands East Indies, with the capture of Java as its ultimate objective, developed along two major routes of advance. In the east, the Japanese drove down through the Philippine archipelago, the east coast of Borneo, the Celebes and other islands towards eastern Java. In the west, they marched south through Malaya to Singapore, secured footholds on the west coast of Borneo and southern Sumatra, and approached Java's western tip.

THE PHILIPPINES

On 10 December, bad weather kept the Kanoya *Ku* Detachment grounded at Taichu, but Takao *Ku* was back over Luzon in full force. Some 27 Type 1s attended to unfinished business from the 8th with a raid on Nichols Field, south of Manila, whilst an identical number hit Del Carmen Field, south of Clark. The latter force was hampered by cloud over the field, however, and they switched their attention to shipping in Manila Bay. During the mission escorting Zeros engaged P-40Es over Manila, decimating the remnants of the US 24th Pursuit Group (PG).

By 12 December the weather over Taiwan and the straits had improved, but parts of Luzon were still under cloud cover. Indeed, when 27 Type 1s from the Kanoya *Kokutai* Detachment were sent to bomb Clark Field, they found the target hidden by cloud, so they unloaded their bombs on Iba instead. Takao *Kokutai's* 52 Type 1 *Rikko* were also redirected against Batangas airfield due to Nichols Field being clouded over.

The following day a total of 104 *Rikko* bombed various targets on Luzon, 26 Kanoya and 26 1st *Ku* machines putting Nichols Field out of commission as an effective base, while 52 aeroplanes from the Takao attacked Olongapo, Iba and Del Carmen. In less than a week the Japanese had established overwhelming air superiority over the Philippines, and worthwhile targets were becoming hard to find.

The *rikko's* long reach was extended to the southern Philippines and beyond when, on 18 December, the Kanoya *Ku* Detachment, with 25 Type 1 *Rikko*, transferred from Taiwan to Peleliu, in the Palau Islands, in order to support landings at Davao scheduled for the 20th. On 21 December, 21 *rikko* of Kanoya *Ku*, flying from their new base at Peleliu, attacked Del Monte Airfield on Mindanao.

On the 22nd the main Japanese invasion force for the Philippines came ashore at Lingayen Gulf, on Luzon. The army made rapid progress following the main landing, with tactical air support provided by its own air units. This left the navy *rikko* still on Taiwan free to go after shipping in Manila Bay between 25 and 28 December.

The G4M crews then switched their attention to the Bataan Peninsula and the island of Corregidor from the 29th onward. Anti-aircraft fire over

Nichols Field is seen under attack by Type 1 *Rikko* of Takao *Kokutai* on 10 December 1941. Originally targeted along with Clark Field on 8 December, this site had been granted a 48-hour reprieve due to poor weather. In a last-minute change in plans, the land attackers were instead directed towards the small coastal strip at Iba. Further bad weather had restricted operations on 9 December, but on the 10th Nichols was badly bombed (*via Edward M Young*)

Corregidor, in particular, was not to be taken lightly, this American strong-hold being the best defended target encountered by the Japanese during the early phase of the Pacific War. Indeed, crews' combat experiences in this area with the G4M led directly to the installation of *Kasei* 15 engines on the Type 1 *Rikko* for better high altitude performance.

During this series of raids flown on 3 January 1942, one Takao machine made a forced landing at Vigan after being hit in the fuel tanks by AA fire, while the following day saw another aircraft shot down by one of the few remaining P-40s on Bataan.

On 28 December 1941 an advance echelon of ten Type 1s of Kanoya *Ku* transferred to the newly-captured airfield at Davao, on the south coast of Mindanao – the rest of the unit followed on 5 January.

The island of Jolo, halfway between Mindanao and northern Borneo was captured on Christmas Day, and between 2-8 January the Takao *Kokutai* transferred 23 of its *rikko* to the airfield there. Although American and Filipino forces continued to hold out on Bataan and Corregidor, the Japanese were leap-frogging to the Dutch East Indies.

MALAYA AND SINGAPORE

With the destruction of *Force Z*, and much of the air support for the army's drive down the Malay Peninsula provided by army air units, the navy's *rikko* in this theatre were mainly employed patrolling the South China Sea, and in support of landings along the west coast of Borneo.

On 16 December 1941, Japanese forces landed at Miri on the north-west coast of Borneo, and from the 18th, the 22nd *Koku Sentai* focused air operations around that island as Allied counterattacks mounted. On 20 December, Kanoya *Ku* Main Body flew a full strength search and attack mission with 26 aircraft, hunting for the elusive airfield from which Dutch air raids on the beachhead at Miri were thought to originate. They found what they were looking for when they discovered Singkawang II near Ledo, and reported bombing 11 large and five small aircraft on the field. A follow up strike on the 22nd by 24 Type 96s from Mihoro *Ku* left the runways temporarily inoperable, forcing withdrawal of the Dutch air units there.

On 24 December, the Japanese landed at Kuching further down the coast from Miri, and captured the airstrip there the following afternoon.

Pre-war Japanese plans to develop Miri and Kuching into major air bases, and to station all of Kanoya *Kokutai* there to support operations against Singapore and western Java did not materialise.

These small fields did not lend themselves easily to expansion, and were not adequately stressed for large aircraft. Unable to station units larger than *Chutai* strength at these fields, the navy was forced to continue operating the bulk of its air units from bases in southern French Indochina. Already at this early date, the limited field engineering capabilities of the Japanese were starting to have an inhibiting effect on their air operations.

The focus of these operations now shifted to Singapore. A reconnaissance overflight by army aircraft on 28 December showed at least 100 aircraft on the island's airfields, prompting the initiation of a joint air campaign by both army and navy air units against the defenders.

The Type 1 *Rikko* made its first appearance over Singapore in the early hours of 3 January when 27 Kanoya aeroplanes bombed Tengah airfield and the navy arsenal. Four days later an army reconnaissance showed that enemy air strength on Singapore had, if anything, been increased, and the air campaign was stepped up.

On the 14th Type 97 fighters (Ki-27 'Nate') of the army's 11th *Hiko Sentai* brought back erroneous reports of an aircraft carrier in Keppel Harbour. The next day 27 Kanoya *Rikko* found no carrier, and bombed Tengah instead, as well as Kluang airfield on the mainland in southern Johore. On the 18th, Kanoya *Ku* was back with 26 aircraft, bombing the oil storage tanks at the western end of the naval base, igniting huge fires.

The air campaign was further intensified in preparation for the army's landings at Cape Endau, in southern Malaya, on 26 January. Five days earlier the Kanoya *Kokutai* sent 27 Type 1s over Tengah, while 25 Mihoro Type 96s went after shipping in Keppel Harbour. Next day 27 Kanoya machines bombed Sembawang airfield, while 25 Genzan *rikko* attacked Kallang.

On both occasions the Type 96s suffered losses at the hands of intercepting Hurricanes, but the Type 1s met no opposition. The superior performance of the Type 1 *Rikko* gave them a distinct advantage over the older Type 96, as Lt(jg) Hajime Sudo of Kanoya *Ku* recalled;

'I always felt kind of sorry for the Genzan and Mihoro boys whenever we flew joint missions with them. On missions to Singapore the idea was to meet up over the target and drop our bombs at about the same time. But flying from the same base, our Type 1 *Rikko* would get there in three-and-a-half hours, faster than the Mihoro aeroplanes by over an hour.

'We would just be leaving our quarters as Mihoro *Ku* would take off. Then, as we approached the target, we would catch up to them straining to maintain 7500 metres altitude as we flew at 8500 with ease. We would then zigzag a few times so they could keep pace with us. Enemy fighters, perhaps scared of our 20 mm tail guns, seldom came after us. If they did, they would make only one pass, then go after the Type 96 *Rikko* formation 1000 metres below and give them hell for a good half-hour.

'The anti-aircraft would concentrate on the lower altitude Type 96s too. We would already be back at base eating ice cream when we would hear the Mihoro formation come home.'

Kanoya *Ku* flew its last mission to Singapore on 27 January, putting 24 *Rikko* over Kallang airfield. Two days later Genzan *Ku* flew the last

Below and bottom
Shown at the peak of the Type 1
Land-Attack Aircraft's combat
career, examples from the 2nd
Chutai of Kanoya *Kokutai* fly in tight
formation during the 'Southern
Advance' in 1942. The letter 'K' in
the aircrafts' serial signified the
Kanoya *Kokutai*, whilst the single
tail stripe and numbers ranging from
316 to 330 indicated 2nd *Chutai*.
These markings did not always
reflect *buntai* personnel
assignments though, for Lt Haruki
Iki, as 3rd *Chutai* leader, normally
flew K-301, which was a 1st *Chutai*
aircraft! He swapped aeroplanes for
the 10 December 1941 attack on
HMS *Repulse*, however, flying K-310,
which was a spare machine of the
1st *Chutai* (*both via R C* Mikesh)

navy bombing mission over the beleaguered island. Thereafter, the reduction of Singapore was left entirely in the hands of the army air force as the *rikko* concentrated on anti-shipping strikes in the surrounding seas. Singapore would surrender on 15 February, but the Japanese were already extending their reach to Sumatra and Java itself.

NETHERLANDS EAST INDIES

The eastern corridor of the main Japanese advance now split into two routes. One route, supported by the Type 1s of Kanoya *Ku* Detachment, the Type 96s of 1st *Ku*, Toko *Ku*'s Type 97 flying boats and the *Rei-sen* of 3rd *Ku*, took Menado on the north-eastern tip of Celebes, Kendari on the island's south-east coast, Makassar on its south-western corner and the island of Bali, adjacent to eastern Java. Also captured were the islands of Ambon and Timor further east. The other route, supported by Takao *Ku* and the *Rei-sen* of Tainan *Ku*, advanced along the east coast of Borneo from Tarakan to Balikpapan, and then to Bandjarmasin on the island's south coast.

Flying from Davao, 14 Type 1s of Kanoya *Ku*, in conjunction with three Type 97 flying boats of Toko *Ku*, attacked Ambon in the pre-dawn hours of 7 January in preparation for landings at Menado on the 11th. The latter was an all-navy operation, which included the IJN's (and Japan's) first use of paratroopers. The Takao *Ku*, flying from its new base at Jolo, bombed Tarakan harbour on 8-9 January in support of army landings, which also took place on the 11th. One aeroplane was lost to anti-aircraft fire on the 8th.

The next stage of the Japanese advance southward was launched on 24 January, when simultaneous landings were made at Balikpapan, on Borneo, and Kendari, on Celebes. Takao *Ku* flew a 35-aeroplane mission against enemy positions at Balikpapan on the day of the landing.

To the east, in response to a reported concentration of enemy aircraft at Ambon, Kanoya *Ku* sent a 26-aeroplane force there on 15 January, returning again the next day with 16 *rikko*. Aside from these one-off bombing raids, G4M crews flying daily patrols over the entire area found little enemy activity, and the landing at Kendari was virtually unopposed. With the capture of Balikpapan, the Japanese seized the richest oil field on Borneo, while at Kendari a huge grass airfield was captured that was capable of immediate use by large numbers of aircraft, including *rikko*.

Meanwhile, the discovery of a secret airfield on Borneo, referred to as Samarinda II by the Dutch, led to it being visited by 43 Takao *Ku* aircraft on 25 January. The *kokutai* returned next day with 35 *rikko*, although bad weather caused 17 of them to turn back before reaching the target, and the rest bombed through cloud. These attacks caused heavy damage to Samarinda II nonetheless, and with the base now bypassed by the Japanese landing at Balikpapan, the Dutch were forced to withdraw the Martin bombers based at the airfield.

Kendari was a godsend for the Japanese, who were finding the airfields at Davao and Jolo inadequate for full-scale operations – the airstrips at Menado, Tarakan and Balikpapan were no better. Kanoya *Ku* Detachment advanced to Kendari on 27 January, moving in less than a week's time from Menado, to which they had deployed from Davao on the 21st. The Type 96 *Rikko* of 1st *Ku* also arrived at Kendari on the last day of the month, and even Takao *Ku*, which was originally meant to operate from other bases, sent 33 of its Type 1s there on 1 February.

The Japanese were now poised to unleash an air superiority campaign against eastern Java. On 3 February a total of 72 *rikko* took off from Kendari and headed for targets on Java. Lt Cdr Nonaka led 26 Takao aircraft to Perak airfield at Surabaya, while 27 Kanoya *rikko*, under the command of Lt Cdr Irisa, headed for Maospati airfield at Madiun. Finally, 19 Type 96s of 1st *Ku* were assigned Singosari airfield at Malang as their target. Damage was done to installations at all three target airfields, as well as Surabaya Naval Base, while between them, the land attackers and the attendant *Rei-sen* destroyed or damaged 38 Allied aircraft. The Japanese lost four *Rei-sen* and one Type 98 Land Reconnaissance Aeroplane.

Crews from both Takao and Kanoya *Ku* fought briefly with a few intercepting fighters, but all returned safely, as did the Type 96s of 1st *Ku*. The Takao *Ku* formation now split up, one *chutai* of nine returning to Kendari with the rest of the *rikko* force, while the remaining 18 headed for Balikpapan, which had finally been prepared for limited *rikko* operations.

On 4 February a Takao *Ku* search aeroplane found the Allied Combined Striking Force in the Flores Sea, and 27 Kanoya, nine Takao and 24 1st *Ku rikko* bombed the ships from medium altitude. Attacking in waves of *chutai* strength, Kanoya *Ku* managed to severely damage USS *Marblehead* with two 250-kg bomb hits and a near miss.

The light cruiser was knocked out of the war for the duration of the Java campaign, being forced all the way back to Brooklyn Navy Yard on the US east coast for major repairs. Bombs from a 1st *Ku* aircraft hit the aft turret of the heavy cruiser USS *Houston*, whilst the same unit put the AA fire control system on the Dutch light cruiser *De Ruyter* out of action with several near misses. During the course of these attacks, a Takao *Ku* G4M commanded by FPO3/c Yasuo Hirata was downed by *Houston's* AA fire.

Although they sank none of the ships, the *rikko* succeeded in turning back the Allied fleet, allowing a successful Japanese landing at Makassar to take place on 9 February.

The Japanese acquired no airfield comparable to Kendari along the western corridor of their advance. The Type 96s of Mihoro and Genzan *Ku* advanced to small forward bases, but with no other adequate fields available, Kanoya *Ku* Main Body remained at Thu Dau Moi. During February, therefore, most *rikko* operations in this sector of the Japanese advance were undertaken by the Type 96s of Mihoro and Genzan *Ku*.

On 14 February army paratroopers, in their first combat operation, descended on Palembang, in southern Sumatra. They secured the airfield and oil field facilities there and linked up next day with regular forces pushing upriver by boat from the coast. The invasion convoy lying off the coast brought out an Allied fleet of five cruisers and ten destroyers, which was spotted near Banka Island on the morning of the 15th. The *rikko* formations bombed the warships but scored no hits. The fleet retreated towards Java nonetheless, unwilling to risk an encounter with Japanese surface forces. At Palembang the biggest oil field in the Indies, as well as a major airfield on the doorstep of western Java, now lay in Japanese hands.

Palembang quickly became crowded with army aircraft, leaving no room for navy *rikko*. As an alternative, the IJN decided to use yet another secret Dutch airfield, discovered by army troops near Gelumbang, 37 km south-west of Palembang. Known to the Allies as Palembang II, or P2, the airfield was used from 24 February onwards by 33 Type 96s and a transport of Genzan *Ku*, as well as 6 Type 1s of Kanoya *Ku*.

Gelumbang, as the field was duly named by its new incumbents, was spacious. But the inability of Japanese logistics to supply the base with adequate fuel stocks in a timely fashion meant that it could only support operations by one *Kokutai* of land attack aircraft at a time. On the 26th, therefore, Genzan *Ku* returned to Kuching, making way for 25 Kanoya *Ku* aeroplanes flying down from Thu Dau Moi. At last the Type 1s in the western sector had secured a good base close to the action.

In the eastern sector of the Japanese advance, the weather closed in on 10 February, and it was not until the 18th that it improved just enough to allow 21 aircraft of Takao *Ku* to attack shipping in Surabaya harbour. For the first time in its combat career, however, the Type 1 *rikko* encountered determined opposition, losing four aircraft.

One machine was destroyed in dramatic fashion by a direct hit from AA fire shortly after dropping its bombs, whilst two others were shot down by P-40Es of the US 17th Pursuit Squadron (Provisional), which for once had received sufficient warning of approaching hostile aircraft, and was well positioned to intercept. The *rikko* of FPO2/c Seiji Miyamoto, badly damaged by the P-40s, ditched in the sea during the return flight. Nine other aircraft sustained damage, including the aeroplane of FPO1/c Katsumi Kitajima, which staggered back to base on one engine having suffered 150 bullet holes, two crewmen dead and two others, including the pilot, FPO2/c Masatomi Ota, wounded.

On 19 February the Japanese landed on Bali, right next to eastern Java, while on the same day the carrier aeroplanes of the 1st Air Fleet launched a devastating raid on Darwin, in north-western Australia. About an hour-and-a-half after the carrier raid, 27 Type 1 *Rikko* of Kanoya *Ku* Detachment and 27 Type 96 *Rikko* of 1st *Ku* added the weight of their bombs to the assault, concentrating on the runways and installations at the Royal Australian Air Force (RAAF) airfield north-east of the town.

These raids were in preparation for landings at Kupang and Dili, on Timor, which took place the next day, placing the Japanese firmly astride the ferry route between Australia and Java.

The encirclement of Java was now complete. As the Japanese intensified their air attacks, it was clear that the island's capture was now merely a matter of time. On 27 February the Japanese spotted a choice target at sea in the form of the seaplane tender USS *Langley*, with two attendant destroyers, making a desperate last minute attempt to transport 33 pilots and 32 P-40s to Tjilatjap, on the south coast of Java.

Lt Jiro Adachi's *chutai* of nine Takao *Ku rikko* fatally damaged the vessel with a perfect pattern of 250-kg and 60-kg bombs, thanks to the careful aim of Adachi's lead bombardier, FCPO Saiji Ozaki. The damage inflicted was too much for the old warship, which was abandoned and finished off by torpedoes and gunfire from the destroyer *Whipple*.

The end now came swiftly for Java. The Allied fleet was destroyed in a series of surface actions between 27 February and 1 March, and on the latter date, the Japanese landed on the island from both east and west. The Dutch command on Java would surrender on 9 March, but with the air campaign already brought to a victorious conclusion, the IJN's *rikko* units began to redeploy elsewhere before the surrender. On 5 March, Kanoya *Ku* Main Body departed Gelumbang and its detachment in the eastern sector left Kendari. With the two halves of the *Kokutai* reunited, the Kanoya returned triumphantly to Japan on 10 March.

However, for the hard-fighting Takao *Kokutai*, there was still work to be done. On 14 March, 18 of its Type 1s transferred to Kupang, on Timor, to begin a campaign against north-western Australia, while two other *chutai* and HQ went to Clark Field, on Luzon, to deal with the stubborn defenders of Bataan and Corregidor. From 24 March Takao *Ku* pounded the latter targets on a daily basis, sharing this work with army Type 97 Heavy Bombers (Ki-21 'Sally'). The AA fire over Corregidor remained as fierce as ever, claiming a *rikko* on 28 March and 2 April.

The conquest of South-east Asia had taken just 90 days. It had cost 19 Type 1 Land-based Attack Aircraft, including operational losses, whilst the casualties among the Type 96 *rikko* were also comparably light. Far to the east, however, there were already disturbing signs that the fight to defend this newly-won empire would be long and hard. And very costly.

HARD LUCK UNIT

Every air force seems to have one – a unit which appears to attract more than its fair share of hardship and misfortune. In the Imperial Japanese Navy the 4th *Kokutai* was such an outfit.

The antecedents of 4th *Ku* go back to the Chitose *Kokutai*'s lonely war in the vast reaches of the Pacific Ocean. While the other units of the *rikko* corps garnered themselves in battle honours as they conquered South-east Asia, Chitose *Ku* struggled to subdue Wake Island, support the capture of Rabaul, on New Britain, and defend its bases in the Marshall Islands against the first probing raids by US carrier forces.

These operations involved Type 96 Land-based Attack Aircraft, which the unit's *rikko* component was largely equipped with. A second Type 1 *Rikko* was ferried out to the Chitose on 15 December 1941 to join Lt Ando's machine, but these aircraft were reserved for single-aeroplane, long distance reconnaissance missions.

On 23 January 1942, the Japanese established themselves in the Bismarck Archipelago following landings at Kavieng, on New Ireland, and Rabaul, on New Britain. Rabaul soon became a key base, serving as the fulcrum for Japanese operations south-west into New Guinea and south-east into the Solomon Islands. Known as the Southwest Pacific Area to the Allies, the region was called the Southeastern Area (*Nanto Homen*) by the Japanese, whose geographic orientation was the opposite of their foes. Plans were laid to establish a new composite unit of land attack aeroplanes and fighters here to undertake air operations in the area.

The *rikko* component of the new unit, to be designated 4th *Kokutai*, was to be made up of three *chutai*. Chitose *Ku*, which had gradually begun to convert to the Type 1 *Rikko*, contributed one *chutai*, commanded by Lt Shigeo Yamagata, while the other two *chutai* came from the veteran Takao *Kokutai*, fresh from their victorious campaign against the Philippines and Dutch East Indies. These were the 4th and 6th *Chutai* of the Takao, led by Lts Masayuki Miyake and Masayoshi Nakagawa, respectively. They had moved back to Takao from Jolo on 31 January with a total of 21 aircraft in preparation for their reassignment, while the rest of Takao *Ku* advanced further south for the campaign against Java.

The two *chutai* departed Takao on 5-6 February and flew via Peleliu to Truk on the 7th. A fatal accident occurred shortly before arrival at Truk, however, when a mid-air collision claimed two aeroplanes and their entire crew, including Lt Miyake. Tragedy had struck even before the new unit had been formed. Lt Yogoro Seto, then with 1st *Ku*'s transport unit, was hastily sent out as Miyake's replacement.

4th *Kokutai* was officially activated on 10 February 1942. While Lt Yamagata's ex-Chitose *Chutai* hurried to complete its transition onto the Type 1 *Rikko* in the Central Pacific, the other two *chutai* advanced to Vunakanau airfield at Rabaul between 14-17 February. Just three days later, on the morning of 20 February, a patrolling Type 97 flying boat of Yokohama *Kokutai* managed to send a contact report of an enemy task force 460 nautical miles from Rabaul before being shot down by its fighters.

This was Vice Adm Wilson Brown's group, centred around the fleet carrier USS *Lexington*, heading for a raid on Rabaul. Rear Adm Eiji Goto, 24th *Koku Sentai* commander, ordered an attack, but torpedoes had not yet been brought to this newly-captured outpost. Neither had auxiliary fuel tanks for the unit's newly-arrived *Rei-sen*, and its obsolescent Type 96 Carrier Fighters could not be counted on for more than local air defence. The 4th *Ku* would have to do their best in a horizontal bombing attack, and they would have to go in unescorted. But the ex-Takao aircrew, flush with recent victories in South-east Asia, were confident and eager to go.

At 1420 on the 20th, 17 Type 1s left Vunakanau, each carrying two 250-kg bombs. The 4th *Ku Hikotaicho*, Lt Cdr Takuzo Ito, was in command as senior observer aboard Lt Seto's G4M, piloted by FCPO Chuzo Watanabe. Seto's lead *chutai* had eight aircraft, while Lt Nakagawa led nine others. The latter found the ships first, and at 1635 radioed he was about to attack. That was the last anyone heard from him and his *chutai*.

Intercepted by F4Fs of VF-3, five *rikko* were downed before getting their bombs away. The remaining four released their bombs against *Lexington* but scored no hits. They were then set upon by Wildcats, which destroyed a further three *rikko* during the withdrawal, although two F4Fs were in turn downed by the G4Ms' 20 mm tail cannon. The last remaining Type 1 of Nakagawa's *chutai* managed to escape the fighters, only to fall victim to an SBD-2 of VB-2.

At 1700 the lead *chutai* also found the carrier, but about five minutes later, as they headed towards their target, they were intercepted by Lt Edward H 'Butch' O'Hare and his wingman Lt(jg) Marion W Dufilho. Dufilho's guns jammed, but in a virtuoso performance, 'Butch' O'Hare downed three *rikko* outright and damaged two others.

One of the damaged G4Ms was that of FPO1/c Koji Maeda, which O'Hare set aflame as the formation approached the bomb release point. On this occasion, however, a hard pull on the fire extinguisher handle did the trick. With the blaze snuffed out, Maeda caught the three other *rikko* still in formation, and the four dropped their 250-kg bombs just wide of the carrier – the closest landed a mere 30 metres astern.

The lead aircraft, with Lt Cdr Ito and Lt Seto both on board, failed to bomb with them, for it had been cut out of formation by O'Hare seconds before bomb release to become his third definite victory of the fight. Fire from the F4F-3 had exploded

This dramatic sequence of photographs, taken from a ciné film shot by a sailor aboard USS *Lexington* during the action of 20 February 1942, shows F-348 (the aircraft of Lt Cdr Takuzo Ito, 4th *Ku Hikotaicho*) desperately attempting to crash into the carrier. The bomber had earlier had its port engine completely blown off during an interception by Lt Edward H 'Butch' O'Hare, flying an F4F-3. The *rikko*'s tail was adorned with two stripes, which indicated a 3rd *Chutai* machine, although with Ito on board, his *chutai* would have been flying the tactical first *chutai* position (*National Archive via Robert C Mikesh*)

the Type 1's port nacelle, blowing the entire engine clean off. In a superb display of flying skill, the pilot managed to right the machine at low level.

During pre-war training the men of the *rikko* corps had agreed that should their aeroplanes be damaged in combat beyond hope of return, they would seek out a target and willingly die in a *jibaku* (self-destruct). Ito now set his sights on the *Lexington* with the lives of his entire crew. But anti-aircraft fire shredded the aeroplane as it approached the carrier, and it finally nosed down and hit the sea at 1712 in a tremendous explosion 1400 metres ahead of *Lexington's* port bow.

One more *rikko* was shot down by another F4F, leaving four still in the air, three in formation and one, flown by FPO1/c Satoshi Mori, seriously damaged by O'Hare, struggling to return home alone. These endured further attacks from both F4Fs and SBDs, but managed to clear the area. The aeroplane of FPO1/c Kosuke Ono, however, was damaged sufficiently in these final encounters to force him to ditch at Nugava, in the Nuguria Islands, at 1925. Twenty-five minutes later, shot to ribbons, the aeroplanes of FPO1/c Maeda and FPO2/c Ryosuke Kogiku landed back at Vunakanau. Finally, at 2010, PO Mori managed to bring his damaged G4M back far enough to ditch in Rabaul's Simpson Harbour.

4th *Ku* had been decimated in its first action, with 88 crewmen dead, including the *hikotaicho* and two *buntaicho*, and 15 out of 17 *rikko* lost. But shocking though the losses were, the Japanese, in their stoicism, simply accepted them at the time as the price which had to be paid in an unescorted attack against the US fleet. It would take countless more dead before the Japanese would reconsider the G4M's vulnerability.

The 1st *Kokutai*, with its older Type 96 *rikko*, was immediately transferred to the theatre to fill the gap, while the sole remaining *chutai* of 4th *Ku*, led by Lt Yamagata, was rushed to Rabaul with ten Type 1 *Rikko* on the 21st. It would not be until the following month that Lt Cdr Hatsuhiko Watanabe would arrive as the new *hikotaicho*, and a new *buntaicho* would arrive in the person of Lt Kuniharu Kobayashi.

Less than two weeks after its formation, 4th *Kokutai* was having to rebuild itself, but the pace of war allowed no respite. On 24 February, with an escort of eight Zeros, Lt Yamagata led nine Type 1s on the unit's first bombing raid against Port Moresby, on the south-east coast of New Guinea. For the 4th *Kokutai*, the war would be long and arduous.

THWARTED OBJECTIVES

The seizing of South-east Asia's natural resources had been the first stage of Japan's grand strategy. Now, in the second stage, it planned to expand the perimeter of its newly won empire to create a buffer zone against an eventual Allied counterattack. This time, things would not go according to plan.

On 10 February 1942, in addition to the formation of the 4th *Kokutai* (see previous chapter), a second new *rikko* unit had also been created. The Misawa *Kokutai* called the base bearing that same name home, the airfield being sited near the northern tip of the main Japanese island of Honshu. Misawa *Ku* was to be composed of three *chutai* equipped with Type 1 Land-based Attack Aircraft, and it began working up to operational status at Kisarazu.

A major reorganisation of naval air units occurred on 1 April 1942, resulting in changes to the size of many *rikko* units, and to their fighter components. To take one example, 4th *Ku* was given a four *rikko chutai* structure, while its fighter component was absorbed by Tainan *Ku*, making the 4th a pure *rikko* unit. Kisarazu *Kokutai* rejoined the ranks of active combat units on this date, with three *chutai* of Type 1 *Rikko*. Its training function was in turn taken over by the Shinchiku *Kokutai*, newly activated on 1 April at Shinchiku (Hsin-chu), on Taiwan.

Also newly formed on 1 April were the 25th and 26th *Koku Sentai*, the former undertaking naval air operations in the Southeastern Area, and the latter originally intended to cover air operations in the north-east. 4th *Ku* came under the control of 25th *Koku Sentai*, while Misawa *Ku* and Kisarazu *Ku* were assigned to the 26th *Koku Sentai*.

On 18 April 1942, the Japanese homeland was bombed by the daring 'Doolittle Raiders', who had flown their US Army B-25s off USS *Hornet*. Although the material damage done by the medium bombers was slight, it shocked military and naval authorities responsible for Japan's protection, and spurred plans already underway to extend the nation's outer zone of defence.

The first major operation of the second stage involved a sea-borne invasion of Port Moresby in order to secure New Guinea, and a landing at Tulagi, in the Solomon Islands.

Close up of the tail of a 4th *Ku* Model 11 damaged at Lae, in New Guinea, during May 1942. The single tail stripe and number in the 320 to 339 range indicate that this aircraft was assigned to the 2nd *Chutai*. The heavy fighting in eastern New Guinea took a steady toll of *rikko* (Al Simmons Collection via Larry Hickey)

This Type 1 Land-based Transport (G6M1-L) of the Tainan *Kokutai* was photographed in the latter half of 1942, probably at Rabaul. Evident in this photo is the port waist gun blister, which was positioned further forward in the transport variant in comparison with the standard *rikko* version – the blister on the starboard side was also located just aft of the wing trailing edge. This was a holdover from the original G6M1 'wingtip escort' design, which incorporated this feature in order to offset the rearward travel of the centre of gravity, caused by the installation of a large ventral gondola housing for two 20 mm cannon (*via S Nohara*)

This would extend Japanese control to the northern end of the Coral Sea, in preparation for an invasion of New Caledonia, Fiji and Samoa in order to cut off America's life line to Australia. In this theatre, the Type 1 *Rikko* of 4th *Kokutai*, supported by the Type 96 *Rikko* of 1st *Ku*, had been continuing its air campaign over New Guinea, supporting the landings at Lae and Salamaua, on the north coast, which had taken place on 8 March 1942.

Although Allied air opposition based in-theatre had been negligible at first, it soon now began to grow in the latter half of the month. Indeed, on the 14 March raid on Horn Island, off the northern tip of Australia's Cape York Peninsula, eight Type 1s and 12 *Rei-sen* of 4th *Ku* tangled with P-40s of the 7th PS/ 49th PG. Two Zeros were lost, but the *rikko* all returned safely.

The land attackers suffered their first combat loss over New Guinea on 21 March when a lone Type 1, piloted by FCPO Heihachi Kawai, failed to return from an afternoon reconnaissance flight to Port Moresby. It had fallen victim to Kittyhawk fighters which had arrived at Port Moresby barely two hours before as part of the advance element of No 75 Sqn RAAF.

With the April reorganisation, the 1st *Kokutai* transferred to the Central Pacific. The air campaign over eastern New Guinea only increased in intensity, however, as 4th *Ku* soldiered on as the sole *rikko* force in the area. Arrival in-theatre of the ace-studded Tainan *Ku* Main Body would provide a major boost to air operations during the month, but by then 4th *Ku* losses had risen considerably.

On 6 April seven *rikko* fought with five enemy fighters, including two P-39Ds of the US 36th PS/8th PG. This was the first time either type had met in combat, and on this occasion all *rikko* returned, although five took hits and one crewman was brought back dead and another badly wounded. Four days later, the 4th *Ku* was back over Moresby again with seven Type 1s, although one was lost to No 75 Sqn. 4th *Ku* was now in danger of having its strength whittled away unless substantial reinforcements arrived – and they were indeed on their way.

10 April 1942 was the official launch date by Combined Fleet of second stage operations, and as part of the redeployment of forces for these operations, the personnel of Tainan *Kokutai* Main Body arrived at Rabaul by ship on the 16th. Their *Rei-sen* had arrived separately, and were expected to be ready by the 20th. The Type 96 *Rikko*-equipped Genzan *Kokutai* was also temporarily assigned to this theatre, and 4th *Kokutai* itself received some replacements in the form of five Type 1 *Rikko*, arriving at Rabaul on 19 April, and eight more on 1 May.

4th *Ku* had renewed its campaign against Port Moresby on 17 April, sending five *rikko* to the target, in company with 13 *Rei-sen*. Eight Type 1s and ten *Rei-sen*, now predominantly flown by pilots of Tainan *Ku*

Main Body, attacked Kila Kila airfield (Three Mile) at Port Moresby on the 21st, all returning safely following air combat.

Thereafter, in almost daily raids on the Moresby area until the end of the month, 4th *Ku* suffering no losses as the Zero pilots of Tainan *Ku* dealt with the steadily dwindling ranks of No 75 Sqn. But in the final days of the month a sizeable contingent of P-39 Airacobras from the US 35th and 36th PSs flew into Seven Mile Strip to relieve the hard-pressed Australians. And in a rare Allied counter-attack, on the afternoon of the 30th, 11 P-39s effectively strafed Lae, burning one *Rei-sen* and wrecking another, holing a further eight Zeros and no less than ten Type 1 *Rikko*.

The month of May opened with renewed efforts to destroy Allied air strength at Port Moresby as Operation *MO* – the seaward invasion of that location – went into high gear. The presence of a US task force lurking in the area was made clear to the Japanese on 4 May when US carrier aeroplanes raided Tulagi, which had been captured unopposed by the Japanese the previous day. No contact was made on the following day, but on the 6th, a Type 97 flying boat of Yokohama *Ku* brought the first definite sighting of the American carriers. During the course of the next two days, the carrier forces of both sides would clash in the historic Battle of the Coral Sea. The part played by the *rikko* units in this engagement, however, was to be marginal.

On the morning of 7 May, following contact reports from cruiser floatplanes and two of their own search aircraft, 4th *Ku* sortied 12 Type 1 *Rikko* armed with Type 91 *Kai* 2 torpedoes from Vunakanau, while Genzan *Ku* contributed 19 Type 96 *Rikko* carrying a pair of 250-kg bombs each. They were not headed for the enemy carriers, however, but towards

The famous ace-filled *Rei-sen* unit Tainan *Ku* employed three Type 1 Transports as squadron hacks in the Southeastern Area during 1942, and at least two of these were destroyed at Buna in a strafing attack by P-400s on 29 August 1942. V-902 was one of those written off, and here it provides the backdrop for battle-weary Allied troops who had just captured the airfield. This photograph was taken in early 1943, and it shows to good advantage the metal fairing covering the gun slit in the tail cone. Note also the lack of small side windows on the lower half of the extreme rear fuselage immediately in front of the tail cone, a feature the Type 1 Land-based Transport shared with other early-production G4M1s (*via Robert C Mikesh*)

Rear Adm J C Crace's cruiser support force near the southern end of Jomard Passage in the Louisiade Archipelago. The two *rikko* units found the enemy warships a little after 1430 and attacked.

As the Genzan formation prepared to enter its bomb run, the ships below suddenly opened fire. The AA barrage was not directed at them, however, but at low level, for 4th *Ku* had commenced its torpedo run. With enemy fire concentrating on the torpedo attack, Genzan *Ku* completed its bomb run and returned to base without loss. 4th *Ku* took 50 per cent losses.

Another shot of the V-902 wreck, which clearly shows the tail markings. Built in November 1940, this aircraft (s/n 613) was the 13th G6M1 completed (*Mat Gac Collection via Larry Hickey*)

In the face of withering fire from the ships, the formation leader, Lt Kuniharu Kobayashi, fell at the head of his men – three other aeroplanes followed in fiery death. Another bomber staggered into Lae with serious damage, while the 'Tail End Charlie' of the formation, commanded by FPO1/c Misao Sugii, managed to ditch at Deboyne Reef with one crewman dead onboard and another seriously wounded. The six remaining aircraft returned to Vunakanau, five of them with damage. Despite their sacrifice, no torpedoes found their mark, and the high level bombing also gained no results.

Although the sinking of USS *Lexington* in the carrier battle fought in the Coral Sea on 8 May gave the Japanese an important tactical victory, the scale of their own carrier air group losses prevented further prosecution of Operation *MO*, and the capture of Port Moresby was postponed to an overland operation scheduled for July.

But the daily grind of air combat over New Guinea continued. The last big raid on Port Moresby in May took place on the 18th, when 4th *Ku Hikotaicho* Lt Cdr Hatsuhiko Watanabe led 16 Type 1 *Rikko* to Seven Mile, while Genzan *Ku* sent 18 Type 96s to the new airfield at Twelve Mile. Over Moresby P-39s of the 35th and 36th FSs (see *Osprey Aircraft of the Aces 36 - P-39 Airacobra Aces of World War 2* for further details) hit the 4th *Ku* formation before the Tainan *Ku* escort could tackle them, destroying one *rikko* and damaging eight others. One of the damaged aeroplanes was written off in a crash landing at Lae, but the rest returned to Rabaul. While the enemy fighters engaged 4th *Ku* and the Zeros, Genzan *Ku* severely damaged Twelve Mile and returned unmolested.

The focus of Combined Fleet's operations now shifted to the Central Pacific. Here, the capture of Midway Island would extend Japanese air patrols towards Hawaii and, it was hoped, lure the US fleet into a decisive engagement. The landing on Midway was scheduled for 6 June (7 June on the Japanese side of the International Dateline). As soon as it was secured, air units, including an advance echelon of nine G4Ms of Misawa *Ku* were to advance to this most eastward of Japanese outposts, with the rest of the Misawa, and its parent 26th *Koku Sentai* HQ, following in July.

The formal orders for this deployment, of course, never came. The destruction of all four Japanese fleet carriers committed to the operation in the epic air-sea battle of 4 June was decisive indeed, but not in the way

V-903 (s/n 209) was also destroyed along with V-902 in the P-400 attack on Buna on 29 August 1942. Before assignment to Tainan *Kokutai*, this machine had been Z-985 of the 1st *Kokutai*. Earlier still, in its original G6M1 configuration, the aircraft is believed to have been tested in the field as an escort gunship (*Mat Gac Collection via Larry Hickey*)

the Imperial Navy had intended. Misawa *Ku* now deployed instead to Saipan, in the Marianas, on 10 July, from where it undertook patrol duties and training.

With the Midway operation cancelled, the focus of activity shifted once again to the Southeastern Area. The need to reorganise Japan's carrier fleet following the debacle at Midway left inadequate naval air forces available for ambitious plans to invade New Caledonia, Fiji and Samoa, and these operations were formally cancelled on 11 July. But the Japanese still hoped to complete their conquest of New Guinea with an overland drive to capture Port Moresby on the south coast, and to consolidate their hold on the Solomon Islands with the construction of an airfield on the island of Guadalcanal, just south of Tulagi.

Following the 18 May raid on Port Moresby, the land attack aeroplanes of 4th and Genzan *Ku* had stood down. Aside from patrol flights, they devoted their time to maintenance and replenishment. In June, Genzan *Ku* sent a daylight raid over Moresby on the first of the month, followed by a series of small night raids thereafter, but the Type 1s of 4th *Ku* continued with their patrol flights during the first two weeks. Bad weather was also a factor in the reduced level of activity.

However, on 16 June 25th *Koku Sentai* reopened the air campaign against Port Moresby with a successful fighter sweep by Tainan *Ku* as Japanese forces geared up for their overland march on the much-bombed town. On the 17th, nine Type 1 *Rikko* of 4th *Ku* were forced to abort their mission due to a severe weather front off Cape Gloucester, but Genzan *Ku* got through with 18 Type 96 *Rikko*, and managed to damage the Australian transport *Macdhui* in Moresby Harbour.

Next day, 18 Type 1s of 4th *Ku*, led by Lt Cdr Watanabe, succeeded in reaching the vessel and effectively finishing off the job started by the Genzan. Although heavy anti-aircraft fire and fighter opposition holed no fewer than 15 *rikko*, they laid down an excellent bomb pattern which doomed the ship. This proved to be the last attack mission flown by the 4th *Kokutai* in June, for the rest of the month was taken up by patrol work. Genzan *Ku* flew one more mission to Port Moresby on 26 June, but then departed the theatre and returned to Japan early the following month, leaving 4th *Ku* on its own once more.

July marked the start of a busy spell for the *rikko*, as the date of the Port Moresby operation neared. On the night of the 3rd/4th, 4th *Ku* sent six bombers out on its first nocturnal raid on Moresby, and on the 5th a major daylight attack was carried out by 20 Type 1s, escorted by 14 Zeros. Considerable damage was done on all these missions, without loss to the *rikko*. A similar sized raid the next day was intercepted by P-39s and P-400s of the 35th FG, and although one crewman was killed in the action, all aircraft returned safely to base.

On the 10th, a major 21-aeroplane raid on Port Moresby was again met with fierce AA fire and fighter interception. The lead aircraft, commanded by Lt Cdr Tadanobu Tsuzaki, 4th *Ku Hikocho* since May, and piloted by *buntaicho* Lt Shigeo Yamagata, was hit by flak and went down shortly before reaching the bomb release point, throwing the formation into confusion, and spoiling its aim. The remaining *rikko* managed to return to Rabaul, but 4th *Ku* had lost two senior officers in one blow.

The initial landing at Buna, on the north coast of Papua New Guinea, took place on 21 July, despite the fact that attempts to suppress enemy air activity at Port Moresby had so far failed. The capricious tropical weather frustrated two attempts to mount major raids on that target on the 18th and 19th, and finally on 20 July – just one day before the landing – 25 Type 1s got through and bombed without loss. A follow up raid on the 24th by 20 *rikko* was the last sizeable mission flown against Moresby in July, although small night raids were undertaken at the end of the month.

DOWN UNDER

With two *chutai* of Type 1 *Rikko* based at Kupang, on Timor, the Takao *Kokutai* began a series of incursions over north-western Australia starting on 16 March 1942. None of these missions were opposed by Allied fighters, and following a raid on Broome on 20 March, the Japanese began sending their *rikko* over without escorts.

This all changed on 28 March, however, when the RAAF airfield at Darwin was attacked by seven unescorted G4Ms. Prior to reaching the target, the *rikko* were intercepted by P-40Es of the US 9th PS/49th PG and suffered one loss. Returning with an escort of 3rd *Ku* Zeros, the bombers flew similar-sized raids on Darwin on the 30th and 31st, but on both occasions no fighters were encountered as the *Rei-sen* pilots fulfilled their task of keeping the P-40s away from the *rikko*.

On 4 April the American fighters were encountered once again north of Darwin, and on this occasion six escorts proved insufficient to ward off attacks on a similar number of *rikko*, the latter losing half their number to the P-40s. Undaunted, Takao *Ku* was back again the next day with seven aeroplanes, escorted this time by a full *chutai* of nine 3rd *Ku Rei-sen*. The force bombed the RAAF airfield without interference.

From 10 April 1942 onwards, Japan entered the second phase of its overall strategy, and its forces in this theatre assumed a defensive stance. Missions over Australia continued, but these were in the nature of suppression and harassment raids, intended to forestall any offensive action against Japanese-held territory.

The other half of Takao *Ku*, which had been pounding Bataan and Corregidor, arrived at Kupang in the latter half of April. But with Allied raids on the base becoming more frequent, a decision was made to withdraw virtually all naval air units in the area to Kendari, on Celebes, keeping Kupang as a staging base for raids on Australia. Before the withdrawal, however, Rear Adm Ryuzo Takenaka, commander of the 23rd *Koku Sentai*, decided to hit Darwin with a major raid. The resulting mission was the toughest ever flown by the Takao *Kokutai* over northern Australia.

On 25 April, three *chutai* of Type 1 *Rikko*, led by Lt Cdr Goro Katsumi, headed for Darwin's RAAF airfield with an escort of 15 *Rei-sen*. Three *rikko* turned back with engine trouble en route to the target, leaving 24 on the bomb run. Despite the presence of the Zeros, the formation was hit by approximately 50 P-40Es from the 49th PG after dropping its bombs, and in a running fight lasting 35 minutes, four land attackers were downed and three others knocked out of formation and left struggling on one engine. One of these ditched 80 nautical miles east of Kupang, while the other two returned to base.

One of these crippled *rikko* was flown by Lt(jg) Takeharu Fujiwara, who managed to stay in formation as the rest of his *chutai* slowed down to cover him. He had four dead crewmen aboard, including his co-pilot, his left engine was shot out, and his G4M was scarred with 180 bullet holes. The bomber was written off in the belly landing which followed, but Fujiwara had made it back to Kupang despite his own serious wounds.

Finally, one of the aeroplanes which had earlier aborted the mission became a total loss when it ditched near the beach in Dili Harbour and caught fire, although the crew was saved. It was not a good day for the Takao. Despite these losses, Takao *Ku* returned to Darwin 48 hours later, and this time the *kokutai's* 16 *rikko* were covered by no less than 21 Zeros – only one aeroplane was claimed by the P-40s on this occasion.

The entire month of May and the early part of June saw Takao *Ku* make good its losses whilst performing routine patrols. Once restored to full strength, the *kokutai* commenced a mini blitz on Darwin starting on 13 June. Some 27 aircraft bombed the town, with identical-strength follow-up raids being undertaken on the 15th and 16th. Escorted by a large fighter force, and bombing from altitudes of 7000 metres and above in order to avoid the P-40s, the *rikko* suffered no aircraft losses, although several G4Ms were hit, and there were casualties among the crew.

July saw air operations in connection with Japanese landings on the Kai, Aru and Tanimbar Islands, to the east of Timor, on the 30th of that month. Takao *Ku* also sent small *shotai*-sized harassment raids over Darwin nightly between 25-30 July, and on that latter date, Lt Cdr Katsumi led 26 Type 1 *Rikko* (with an escort of 26 *Rei-sen* from 3rd *Ku*) on a daylight attack on the town's airfield. The only loss suffered by the force was a Zero downed by a P-40. In a separate raid flown that same day, nine *rikko* attacked Port Hedland, in Western Australia, without incident.

In August, as in July, the *rikko* flew just one daylight mission to Darwin. On the 23rd, 27 G4Ms (led by Lt Tanemasa Hirata) struck Hughes and other new satellite airfields south of Darwin, destroying fuel and ammunition dumps and two aircraft. Radar gave ample warning of their approach, however, and 24 P-40s of the 49th FG were ready and waiting.

Despite being escorted by 27 Zeros, the *rikko* were attacked several minutes prior to commencing their bomb run. One G4M fell in flames and another had an engine shot out, although this second machine was saved by the Zero escort and made it back to Dili, where it crash-landed. The rest of the bombers fought their way through to the target, and soon after releasing their ordnance, two others received serious damage, although they returned to Kupang. The action had lasted an entire hour.

Although Takao *Ku* had limited its losses to one crew and two aircraft, four escorting Zeros had been destroyed. These casualties put an end to daylight raids over the Darwin area for the rest of the year, and Takao *Ku* switched to nuisance raids at night. Far more serious trouble was brewing in the Solomon Islands, far to the east.

GUADALCANAL – FUNERAL PYRE OF THE *RIKKO*

In the Southeastern Area, August 1942 opened with 25th *Koku Sentai* focused on supporting the overland drive to take Port Moresby. Early on the morning of 7 August, 27 Type 1 *Rikko* of 4th *Kokutai* made ready at Rabaul to attack a newly discovered enemy airfield at Milne Bay, on New Guinea's eastern tip. Before they could depart on their mission, however, crews received the shocking news of enemy landings in the Solomon Islands. US Marines had overwhelmed the small garrison on Tulagi, and on the island of Guadalcanal to the south, easily capturing the small airstrip just completed by Japanese construction troops.

The raid on Milne Bay was hastily changed to a search and attack mission against the US task force in the Solomons, 560 nautical miles from Rabaul. With no time to change their ordnance to torpedoes, the 27 *rikko* took off with a combination of 250- and 60-kg bombs at 1006 and headed for the US ships, escorted by 17 Zeros from Tainan *Ku*. Led by Lt Rempei Egawa, the formation reached Guadalcanal shortly after 1300.

Having received no information on the location of enemy carriers, and seeing none, Egawa decided to go after a cruiser and other vessels near Guadalcanal. The Type 1s committed themselves to their run just as they came under fire from F4Fs and ships' AA. In the ensuing action, four *rikko* were downed, one ditched on the way home and another was lost in a crash-landing at Rabaul. But the American ships had not even been scratched, and the task force continued to lurk somewhere in the area.

The next morning 4th *Ku* went back, this time properly armed with torpedoes. Led by Lt Shigeru Kotani, 17 *rikko* took off from Vunakanau, joined by nine aeroplanes from Misawa *Kokutai's* 2nd *Chutai*, under Lt Hiromi Ikeda. These aircraft had been rushed down to Rabaul from Saipan the previous day following news of the enemy landings. Three 4th *Ku rikko* aborted, leaving 23 target-bound.

Hastily photographed from the deck of a US naval vessel off Guadalcanal, Type 1 *Rikko* F-311 of the 1st *Chutai*, 4th *Kokutai* is seen shortly after dropping its torpedo during the disastrous 8 August 1942 attack. Of the 23 G4Ms which made the attack, only five returned to base. This was the worst single loss of Type 1 *Rikko* during the entire Guadalcanal campaign (*National Archive via J F Lansdale*)

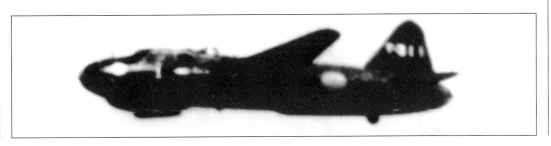

With an escort of 15 *Rei-sen*, the land attackers went after the shipping off Guadalcanal, as search aeroplanes had once again failed to find the carriers. The *rikko* arrived on target shortly before noon, but as they dropped down to wave-top height to begin their runs, the anti-aircraft fire from Rear Adm Kelly Turner's screening force of cruisers and destroyers proved absolutely ferocious. At least eight land attackers fell to the ships' guns in quick succession, and only a few managed to drop torpedoes.

As the survivors withdrew they were set upon by F4Fs, and four more fell in flames. In the end only five severely damaged *rikko* (three 4th *Ku*, and two Misawa) returned to Rabaul. Another Misawa aeroplane crashed and the crew was recovered, but the remaining 11 from 4th *Ku* and six from Misawa had gone down with 125 men, including all the officers. It was to be the worst single loss of *rikko* during the entire Guadalcanal campaign. Only one torpedo had found its mark, damaging the destroyer USS *Jarvis*, while Reserve Lt(jg) Takafumi Sasaki, in his death dive, had ploughed into the transport USS *George F Elliott*, setting the ship on fire.

The afternoon of the 8th saw the arrival at Vunakanau of the remaining 17 Type 1 *Rikko* of Misawa *Kokutai*. The following morning, 16 torpedo-armed Misawa *rikko* went out in search of the elusive US task force, but found only the destroyer *Jarvis*, damaged the previous day, steaming alone. Mistaking her for a cruiser, they sank the ship with two torpedoes, but paid a heavy price for such a small target.

Anti-aircraft fire from *Jarvis* destroyed two *rikko* manned by veterans of the attack on battlecruiser *Repulse* at the start of the war, and damaged a third which crash-landed on Buka. The destroyer perished with all hands, leaving only her enemies to pay tribute to her gallant end.

That afternoon, the US convoy pulled out from the invasion area. Although unloading had not been completed, their departure had been hastened by the American defeat in the cruiser action off Savo Island the night before. Thus, on the morning of the 10th, Japanese aircraft found no ships off Tulagi or Guadalcanal. This caused the Japanese command to overestimate the effectiveness of their attacks, made at such great sacrifice. It was now concluded that enemy forces remaining on Guadalcanal and Tulagi were few in number and low in morale. The resulting piecemeal commitment of forces to deal with them began a bloody six-month battle of attrition which would ultimately defeat Imperial Japan.

Underestimation of the enemy at Guadalcanal also led to a decision to continue the overland drive on Port Moresby as scheduled. With the 4000-strong main force of the South Seas Detachment about to land near Buna, Lt Tomo-o Nakamura, Misawa *Ku Hikotaicho*, led 16 Misawa and nine 4th *Ku* aircraft to Seven-Mile Drome on 17 August.

This well-known flying shot of a 4th *Ku* Type 1 of the 1st *Chutai* was taken during the late summer of 1942. The lack of tail stripes, and a tail number in the 301 to 319 range, indicate that this is a 1st *Chutai* machine. The aircraft is in reconnaissance or ferrying mode, with fairing panels making the bomb-bay flush with the fuselage undersurface. Propeller spinners were introduced on the G4M from July of that year onwards (*Dr Yashuo Izawa via Larry Hickey*)

Bombing from 7000 metres without interference from enemy fighters, the *rikko* destroyed 11 aircraft on the ground in one of their most effective raids on this much visited target. They also destroyed the operations building, burned 200 drums of fuel and left more than a score of 250-kg bombs with delayed action fuses strewn about the runway. Helped also by bad weather, South Seas Detachment was able to disembark next day completely undisturbed by Allied aircraft.

On Guadalcanal, the 916-man advance party of the Ichiki Detachment landed on 18 August, but in its headlong rush to attack what was thought to be a small enemy force, the Japanese troops were slaughtered in the Battle of the Tenaru River on the night of 20/21 August.

The following day Kisarazu *Kokutai* arrived in-theatre, initially with 19 Type 1 *Rikko* based at Kavieng – 24 hours earlier, the Americans had also flown in the first F4Fs and SBDs to the airfield at Guadalcanal, which they named Henderson Field. There were now three *kokutai* of Type 1 Land-based Attack Aircraft in the Rabaul area, but such was the rate of attrition that composite formations quickly became the norm.

On 25 August, Lt Miyoshi Nabeta (veteran of the Kanoya's attack on the *Prince of Wales*, and now Kisarazu *Ku Hikotaicho*) led 23 *rikko* – nine from Kisarazu, eight from Misawa and six from the 4th – in an attack on Henderson Field, from which all the bombers returned unscathed. The airfield was struck again the next day when Lt Nakamura led eight *rikko* each from the Misawa and Kisarazu *Ku*. The land attackers burned 2000 gallons of aviation fuel, which in turn cooked off two 1000-lb bombs and damaged several aircraft on the ground, as well as the field radio station. This time the *rikko* were intercepted by F4Fs of VMF-223 after bomb release, and two Kisarazu aeroplanes were shot down, a third was forced to ditch and Lt Nakamura himself had to make a forced-landing at Buka.

On the 29th, Kisarazu *Ku* lost one aircraft shot down and another crash-landed at Buka out of nine sent to Henderson Field, while nine others from Misawa *Ku* suffered no loss. On the 30th, Lt Nabeta went after shipping off Guadalcanal with 18 *rikko* (nine Kisarazu, nine Misawa) and sank the converted destroyer-transport USS *Colhoun* with a perfect pattern of bombs, returning home without loss in the bargain.

Misawa *Kokutai* Model 11s are seen during the deployment to Saipan on 10 July 1942. A month later the unit became embroiled in the fighting for Guadalcanal following its hasty move to Rabaul, New Britain. The two aircraft closest to the camera (H-362 and H-351) are newer machines in overall green uppersurface camouflage, and belong to the 3rd *Chutai*, as evidenced by the broad vertical tail band. A number of 2nd *Chutai* aircraft can also be seen in the background, with broad horizontal tail bands. These are still painted in the older green and brown 'China Scheme', and exhibit considerable weathering on the original print. This indicates that they were 'hand-me-downs' from Kanoya *Kokutai*, which provided most of the men and equipment for the formation of Misawa *Ku* (via S Nohara)

September saw renewed efforts against Guadalcanal, as air strikes were stepped up in preparation for another ground offensive. On the 2nd, Lt Nabeta was back over Henderson with nine *rikko* each from the Kisarazu and Misawa, returning without loss despite a scrap with F4Fs.

On the same day, Lt Nobuo Ando arrived at Vunakanau with a detachment of ten Type 1s from Chitose *Kokutai* for a two-week tour at Rabaul.

Even with reinforcements, units in the Southeastern Area were becoming dangerously overstretched. While the Japanese concentrated on Guadalcanal, growing Allied air strength in Australia put ever increasing pressure on the Japanese effort in New Guinea. Without sufficient air strength to prosecute the air war simultaneously over both New Guinea and the Solomons, a Japanese concentration of effort in one theatre gave respite to the enemy in the other.

The air campaign in the region was bringing numerous Japanese weaknesses into sharp focus, with a shortage of airfields in the area greatly restricting operational effectiveness. Forced to fly exclusively from Rabaul and Kavieng, *rikko* crews and fighter pilots could undertake just a single six-and-a-half-hour mission a day to Guadalcanal. Moreover, the fickle tropical weather frequently forced aircraft to turn back, dissipating the vital concentration of follow-up air strikes.

The most serious problem, however, was the vulnerability of the Type 1 *Rikko* itself, and it was during the Guadalcanal campaign that the aircraft was saddled with the unwelcome, but sadly appropriate, sobriquet of 'One-shot Lighter'. The Type 1's incendiary properties forced them to bomb at ever higher altitudes in an effort to avoid Henderson's 90 mm anti-aircraft guns, as well as its fighters.

Earlier in the year, standard bomb runs over Port Moresby had settled into a glide-bombing pattern which commenced at 7500 metres and saw the ordnance released at 7000 metres, and at a diving angle of five degrees. Now, over Guadalcanal, the preferred altitude was over 8000 metres (26,000 ft.). At that height, moisture in the crews' oxygen masks froze.

Finally, there was the matter of the warrior ethos by which the airmen flew and fought. While needless loss of life was never part of their code, the martial traditions of the nation exhorted all those bearing arms to embrace death willingly when it came. Added to this was the mortal prohibition in the Imperial armed forces against capture by the enemy – a fate worse than death.

While *rikko* crews shared with their brethren the world over the familiar drama of bomber combat in World War 2, one thing they would not do was bail out over enemy territory. In a conscious decision to forsake this option, the men of the land attack corps (*continued on page 62*)

A Model 11 of the Kisarazu *Kokutai* overflies the Solomon Islands in August or September 1942. Along with the Kanoya *Kokutai* (the oldest unit in the *rikko* corps), Kisarazu *Ku* garnered many battle honours during the early phase of the war in China, flying Type 96 *Rikko*. After several years as a training unit, the Kisarazu returned to combat duty in April 1942, only to find itself decimated in the Guadalcanal campaign that autumn (*Bunrindo K K*)

COLOUR PLATES

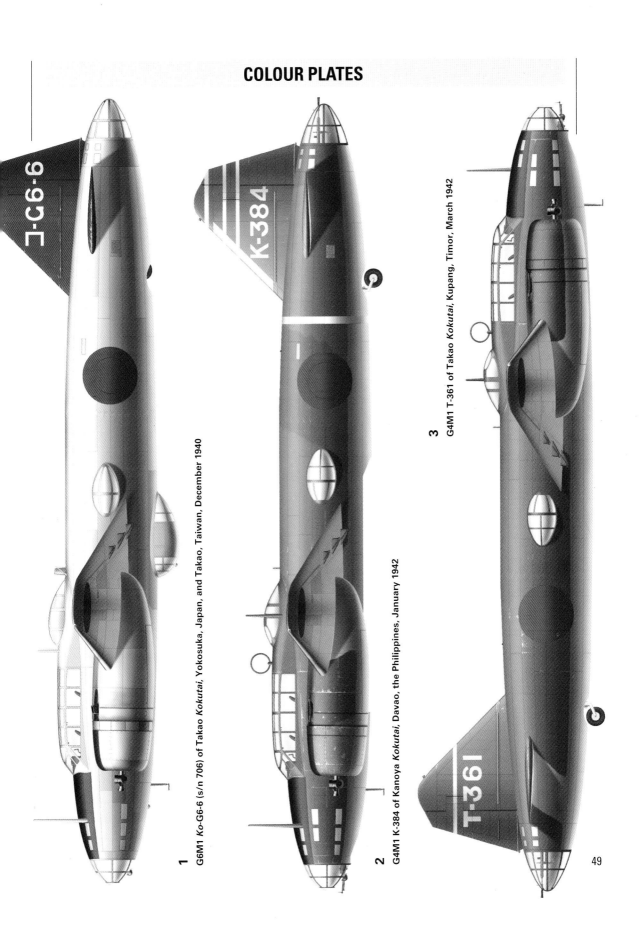

1
G6M1 *Ko*-G6-6 (s/n 706) of Takao *Kokutai*, Yokosuka, Japan, and Takao, Taiwan, December 1940

2
G4M1 K-384 of Kanoya *Kokutai*, Davao, the Philippines, January 1942

3
G4M1 T-361 of Takao *Kokutai*, Kupang, Timor, March 1942

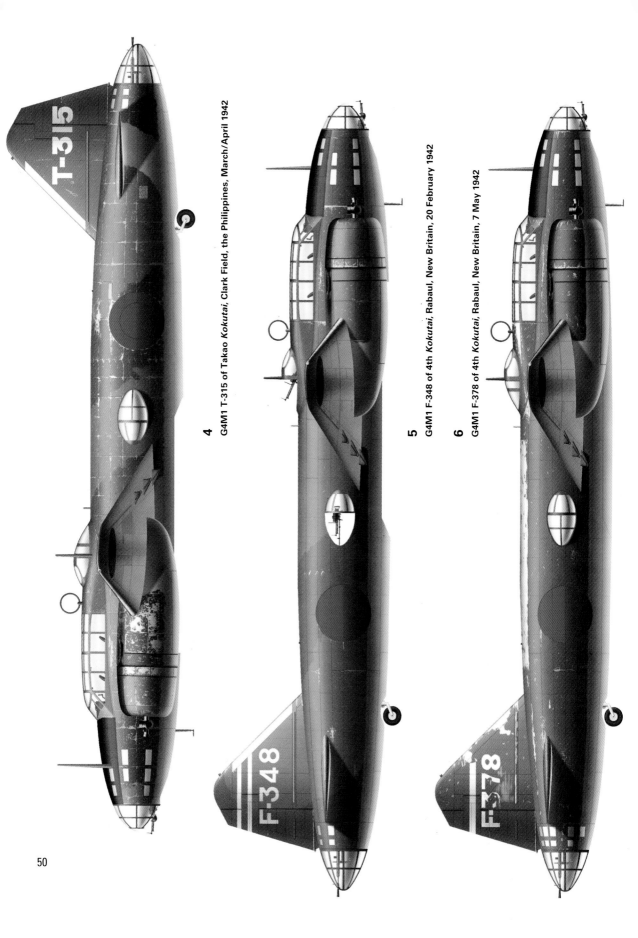

4

G4M1 T-315 of Takao *Kokutai*, Clark Field, the Philippines, March/April 1942

5

G4M1 F-348 of 4th *Kokutai*, Rabaul, New Britain, 20 February 1942

6

G4M1 F-378 of 4th *Kokutai*, Rabaul, New Britain, 7 May 1942

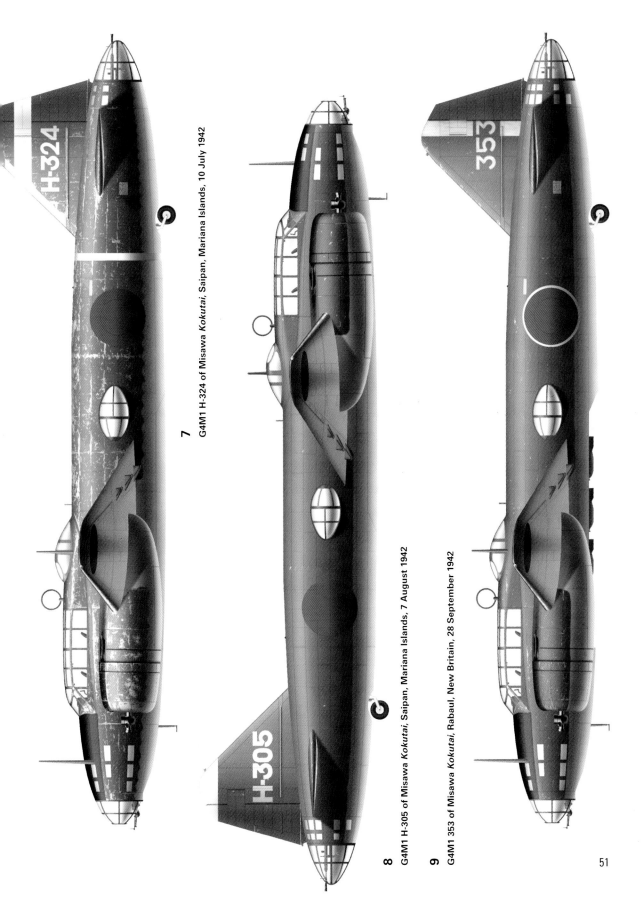

7

G4M1 H-324 of Misawa *Kokutai*, Saipan, Mariana Islands, 10 July 1942

8

G4M1 H-305 of Misawa *Kokutai*, Saipan, Mariana Islands, 7 August 1942

9

G4M1 353 of Misawa *Kokutai*, Rabaul, New Britain, 28 September 1942

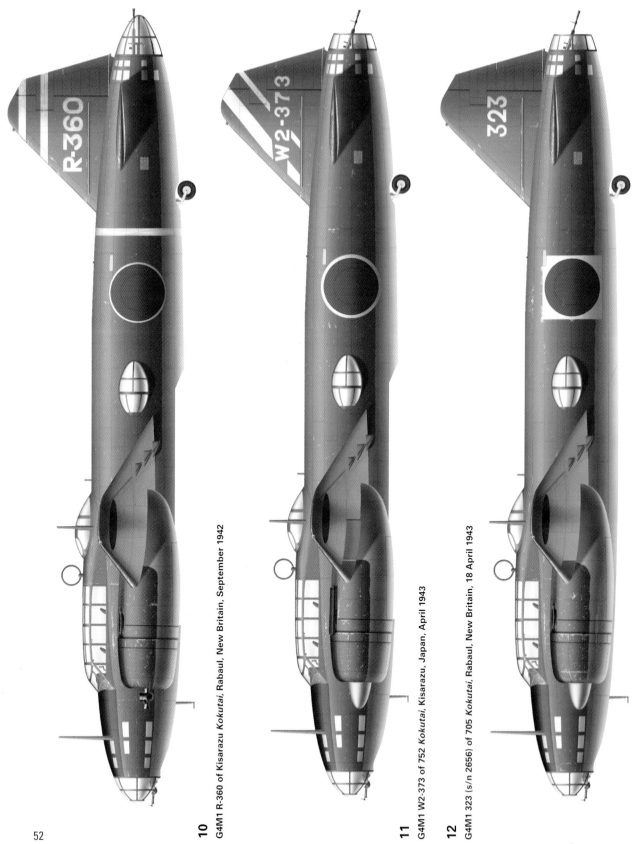

10

G4M1 R-360 of Kisarazu *Kokutai*, Rabaul, New Britain, September 1942

11

G4M1 W2-373 of 752 *Kokutai*, Kisarazu, Japan, April 1943

12

G4M1 323 (s/n 2656) of 705 *Kokutai*, Rabaul, New Britain, 18 April 1943

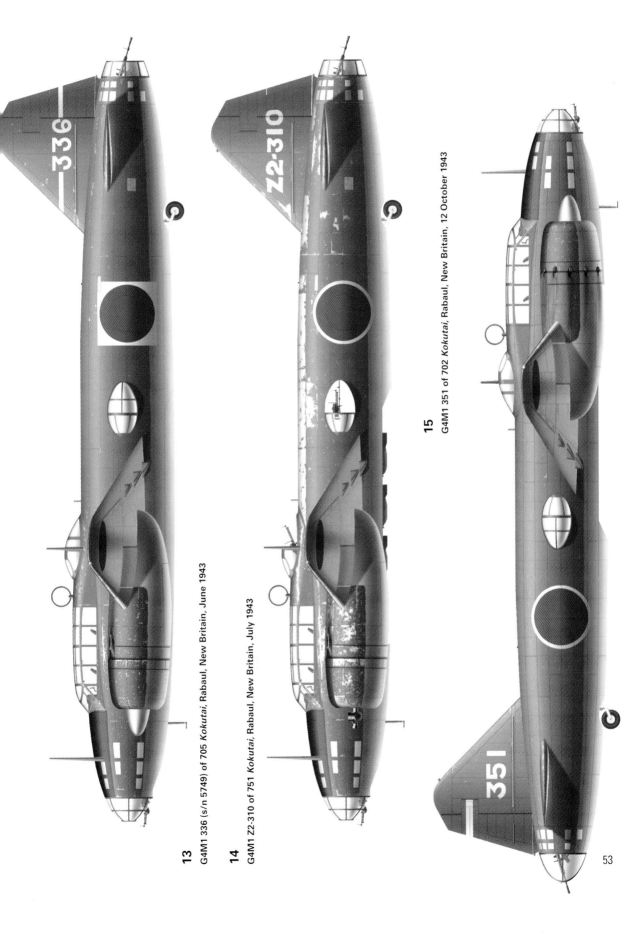

13
G4M1 336 (s/n 5749) of 705 *Kokutai*, Rabaul, New Britain, June 1943

14
G4M1 Z2-310 of 751 *Kokutai*, Rabaul, New Britain, July 1943

15
G4M1 351 of 702 *Kokutai*, Rabaul, New Britain, 12 October 1943

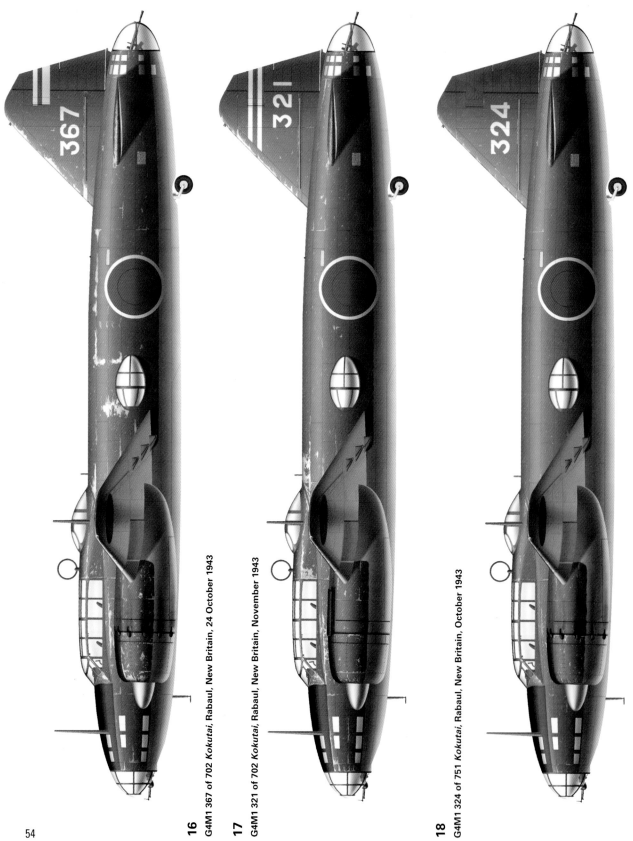

16
G4M1 367 of 702 *Kokutai*, Rabaul, New Britain, 24 October 1943

17
G4M1 321 of 702 *Kokutai*, Rabaul, New Britain, November 1943

18
G4M1 324 of 751 *Kokutai*, Rabaul, New Britain, October 1943

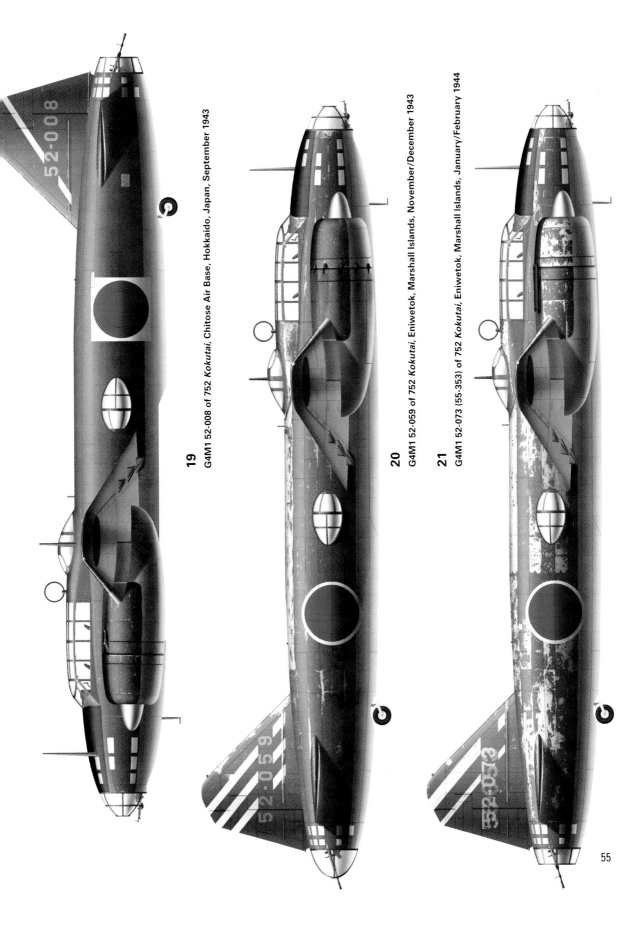

19
G4M1 52-008 of 752 *Kokutai*, Chitose Air Base, Hokkaido, Japan, September 1943

20
G4M1 52-059 of 752 *Kokutai*, Eniwetok, Marshall Islands, November/December 1943

21
G4M1 52-073 (55-353) of 752 *Kokutai*, Eniwetok, Marshall Islands, January/February 1944

22

G4M2 *Ryu 41* of 761 *Kokutai*, Peleliu, Palau Islands, March 1944

23

G4M2 06-303 of 706/755 *Kokutai*, Truk, Caroline Islands, March/April 1944

24

G4M2 01-312 of 701/755 *Kokutai*, Guam, Mariana Islands, April 1944

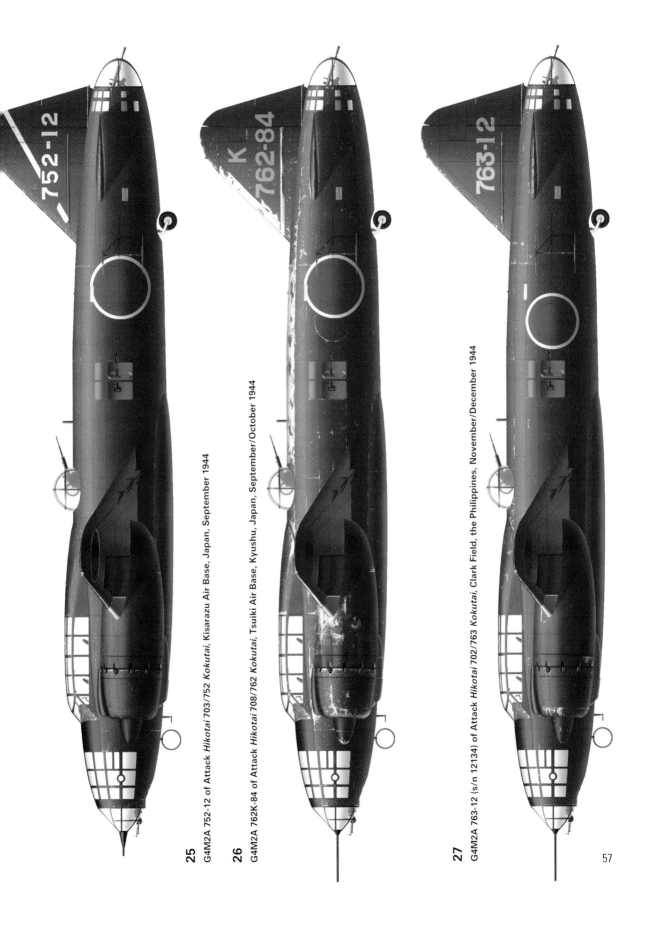

25

G4M2A 752-12 of Attack *Hikotai* 703/752 *Kokutai*, Kisarazu Air Base, Japan, September 1944

26

G4M2A 762K-84 of Attack *Hikotai* 708/762 *Kokutai*, Tsuiki Air Base, Kyushu, Japan, September/October 1944

27

G4M2A 763-12 (s/n 12134) of Attack *Hikotai* 702/763 *Kokutai*, Clark Field, the Philippines, November/December 1944

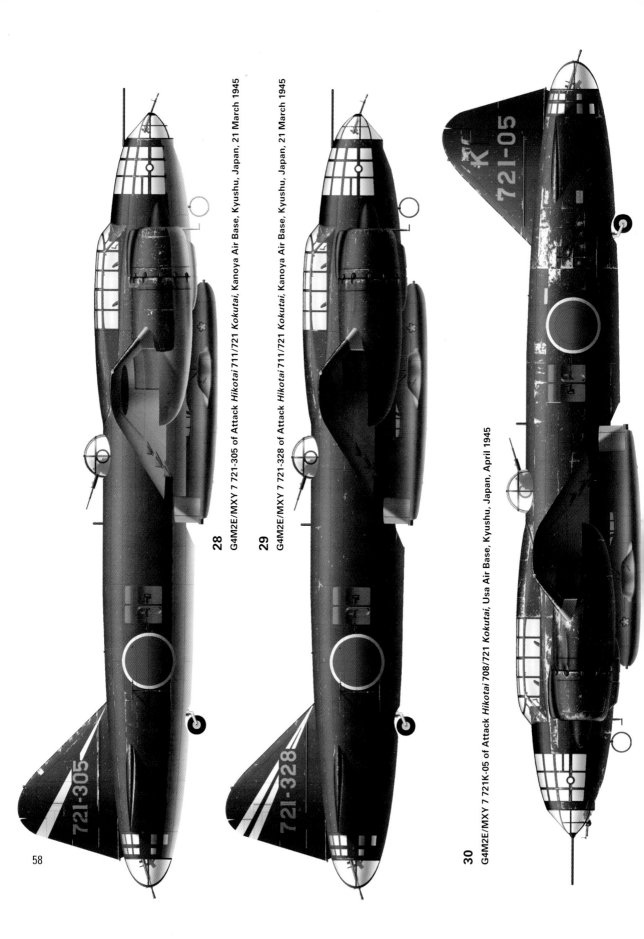

58

28

G4M2E/MXY 7 721-305 of Attack *Hikotai* 711/721 *Kokutai*, Kanoya Air Base, Kyushu, Japan, 21 March 1945

29

G4M2E/MXY 7 721-328 of Attack *Hikotai* 711/721 *Kokutai*, Kanoya Air Base, Kyushu, Japan, 21 March 1945

30

G4M2E/MXY 7 721K-05 of Attack *Hikotai* 708/721 *Kokutai*, Usa Air Base, Kyushu, Japan, April 1945

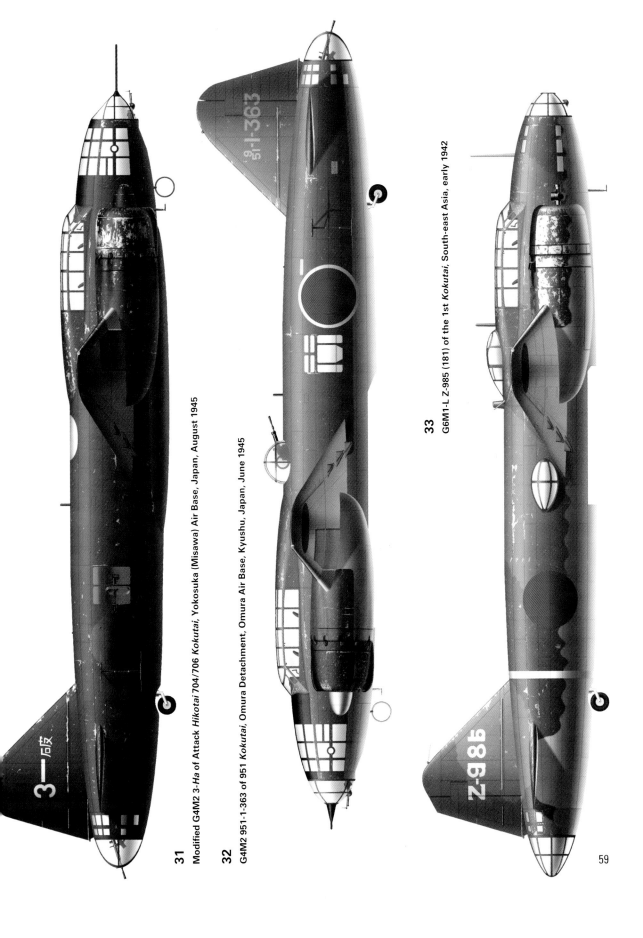

31

Modified G4M2 3-*Ha* of Attack *Hikotai* 704/706 *Kokutai*, Yokosuka (Misawa) Air Base, Japan, August 1945

32

G4M2 951-1-363 of 951 *Kokutai*, Omura Detachment, Omura Air Base, Kyushu, Japan, June 1945

33

G6M1-L Z-985 (181) of the 1st *Kokutai*, South-east Asia, early 1942

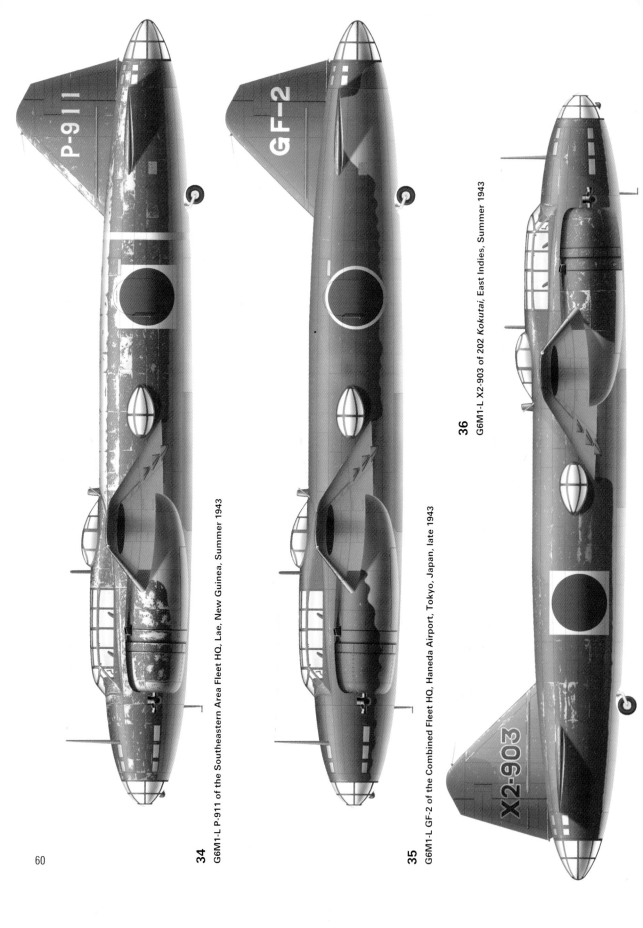

34

G6M1-L P-911 of the Southeastern Area Fleet HQ, Lae, New Guinea, Summer 1943

35

G6M1-L GF-2 of the Combined Fleet HQ, Haneda Airport, Tokyo, Japan, late 1943

36

G6M1-L X2-903 of 202 *Kokutai*, East Indies, Summer 1943

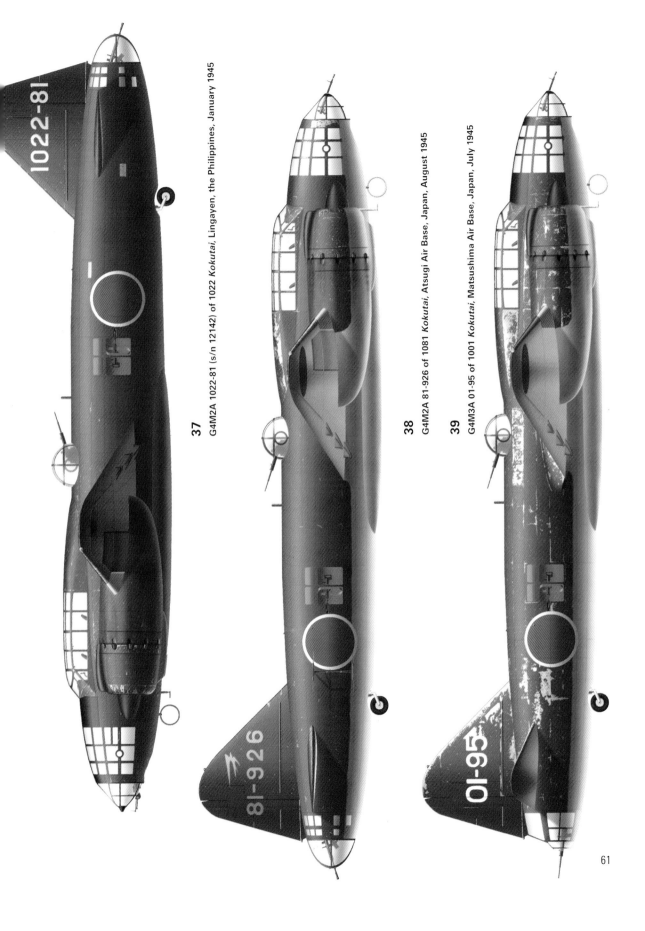

37
G4M2A 1022-81 (s/n 12142) of 1022 *Kokutai*, Lingayen, the Philippines, January 1945

38
G4M2A 81-926 of 1081 *Kokutai*, Atsugi Air Base, Japan, August 1945

39
G4M3A 01-95 of 1001 *Kokutai*, Matsushima Air Base, Japan, July 1945

carried no parachutes on combat missions. All too often, in the thick of the fight, a final wave or salute from a burning cockpit was the last anyone would see of a seven-man team on its final plunge.

Daylight raids on Guadalcanal reopened on 9 September with a 25-aeroplane attack on shipping in Sealark Channel. A *rikko* each from the Chitose and Misawa *Ku* failed to return, while one Kisarazu machine crash-landed on Buka. On the 10th, the Misawa had one aeroplane shot down, two others posted missing and another force-landed at Buka, while a Kisarazu aeroplane ditched at Rekata Bay, on Santa Isabel, where the Japanese had just established a seaplane base four days earlier.

On the 12th, out of 25 *Rikko* attacking Henderson Field (nine Kisarazu, 11 Misawa and five Chitose), two Kisarazu and two Misawa machines were lost directly to enemy action, while a Kisarazu aeroplane came down at Buka and a Chitose *Ku* machine ditched at Rekata. But the day also brought welcome reinforcements, as an advance party of nine Type 1s from the Kanoya *Kokutai* arrived at Rabaul.

The next day the newly-arrived unit took part in its first mission over Guadalcanal in company with eight Kisarazu, seven Misawa and two Chitose machines. Bombing what the Japanese erroneously thought were enemy artillery positions at Taivu Point, one Kisarazu aeroplane was posted missing and another ditched at Rekata.

On the night of 13/14 September, a furious second attempt to retake Henderson Field ended in failure. Despite this defeat, Imperial General Headquarters in Tokyo decided that Guadalcanal would be retaken at any cost. Accordingly, on 16 September the two remaining Type 1-equipped *Chutai* of Kanoya *Ku* arrived at Kavieng, and the detachment at Rabaul transferred there to join them. On the 23rd, a two-*Chutai* detachment from the Takao *Kokutai* flew into Rabaul from the East Indies with 20 Type 1s to lend its support.

These reinforcements meant that the Chitose *Ku* Detachment could return to the Marshalls and the exhausted survivors of 4th *Ku* sent home. Between the 25th and the end of the month, the few survivors of 4th *Ku* and their six remaining *rikko* made their way back to Kisarazu. In seven months of combat, the ill-starred 4th *Kokutai* had lost two *Hikotaicho* in succession, six *buntaicho*, over 40 crews and more than 50 aircraft.

Meanwhile, in New Guinea, the men of the South Seas Detachment had slogged across the forbidding barrier of the Owen Stanley Mountains and reached the last ridge line before Port Moresby by mid-September. But with the Guadalcanal campaign going badly, they were ordered to fall back, and in the face of mounting enemy resistance, shorn of air support and short of food, they began a bitter withdrawal on 25 September.

Bad weather prevented raids on Guadalcanal for nearly two weeks in the latter half of September. During this time support was given to the neglected New Guinea theatre, with night raids on Port Moresby on the 17th and 19th, and a major daylight raid by 27 *rikko* on the 21st. Eight Misawa G4Ms also dropped supplies at Kokoda, in the Owen Stanleys, on the 23rd, but these efforts were not enough to prevent the withdrawal.

On 27 September, the land attackers finally went back to Guadalcanal. Lt Nabeta led eight from his Kisarazu *Ku*, as well as nine from the newly-arrived Takao *Ku* Detachment flying their first mission in-theatre. One Takao aeroplane was shot down and another ditched at Rekata, while the

Kisarazu also lost an aeroplane to enemy fighters. In return, the *rikko* men damaged five SBDs, five TBFs and six F4Fs on the field, and discovered a new airfield to the east of Henderson, known to the Americans as 'Fighter One'. But the 28th brought disaster when Lt Rinji Morita of the Misawa led 25 *rikko* over Henderson Field and Lunga Point.

Intercepted by 35 F4Fs from VMF-223, VMF-224 and VF-5 prior to bomb release, the land attackers missed their target as their formation was shredded and Morita's lead aeroplane taken out. In all, four Takao *rikko*, plus Morita's G4M from the Misawa, went down. Three Kanoya aircraft were also lost, one ditching at Rekata, another crash-landing at Buin (a new airfield not yet completed in southern Bougainville) and a third being scrapped upon its return due to battle damage.

Such heavy losses in just two days called for a change in tactics, and on the 29th nine Kisarazu aeroplanes acted as decoys for a fighter sweep, turning back after guiding 27 *Rei-sen* as far as the Russell Islands.

In the midst of all this action, a complete redesignation of the navy's combat air units took place between 20 September and 1 November. Each was given a three-digit numerical identity in place of the previous base name or single or double-digit numbers. The vast majority of units made the switch on 1 November, but the Kanoya and Takao *Kokutai* were redesignated on 1 October. *Rikko* units were given numbers in the 700s range, the Kanoya being redesignated 751 and the Takao 753.

Although night raids by *rikko* crews against Guadalcanal had started as early as 29 August, they now became more frequent as the Japanese tried to maintain some kind of pressure against the Americans, while limiting their own losses. The worn out and often unsynchronised *Kasei* engines droning over Henderson Field at night became a familiar sound to the US Marines. 'Washing Machine Charlie', one of the enduring icons of the war in the South Pacific, had been born.

But nocturnal nuisance raids alone would not win Guadalcanal back from the 'Yankee devils'. Starting on 11 October, the *rikko* formations returned to Guadalcanal in a series of major daylight attacks as part of a climactic effort to retake Henderson Field. And with the airfield at Buin now operational, at last more than one strike could be flown per day.

On the 11th, however, thick cloud cover over the target hampered their efforts. Out of 45 Type 1s sent to Guadalcanal that day (the strongest force to date), only the 18 aeroplanes of 751 *Ku*, led below the cloud ceiling by their *Hikotaicho*, Lt Cdr Kazuo Nishioka, managed to drop bombs. These fell wide of the mark, and in a scrap with F4Fs, 751 lost one shot down and another crash-landed at Buin.

On the morning of the 13th, Lt Shigeji Makino of 753 *Ku* Detachment led a composite formation of 25 Type 1 *Rikko* over both Henderson and the new fighter strip. With no enemy interference, the land attackers ploughed up the fields, destroyed a B-17 and damaged a dozen other aircraft, as well as setting fire to 5000 gallons of aviation fuel – one 753 *rikko* ditched at Rekata with damage. In the afternoon, 14 Type 1s of 751 *Ku* bombed Henderson and returned without loss.

On the night of 13/14 October, Henderson received its greatest pounding of the entire campaign when the IJN battleships *Kongo* and *Haruna* rained 14-inch shells on the field for over an hour. This left the airfield in smoking ruin.

Shortly after midday on the 14th, 26 Type 1s (eight Kisarazu, nine Misawa and nine 753) bombed both Henderson and 'Fighter One' without opposition. However, a follow-up strike by 12 aeroplanes of 751 *Ku* unexpectedly met enemy fighters – the stubborn aerial defenders of Guadalcanal had not been exterminated. Three *rikko* were shot down and a fourth just managed to ditch at Rekata. On the 15th, 23 land attackers (six 753, nine Misawa and eight Kisarazu) bombed without interference, although anti-aircraft fire holed as many as 14 aeroplanes, and caused one to ditch in Simpson Harbour at Rabaul.

The land attackers now turned their attention to enemy troop positions in preparation for the big push by 17th Army against the Americans. 17 October saw 18 *rikko* attack positions around Lunga River, losing one Kisarazu aeroplane ditched at Rekata, while the next day, in a tough encounter with F4Fs, 15 *rikko* bombed positions west of the river. Two Misawa aeroplanes were downed and a third crash-landed with damage.

On the 20th, nine aeroplanes from 753 suffered no losses in a brief engagement with Wildcats, while the next day nine Kisarazu *rikko* also returned intact. On the 23rd, however, 16 land attackers lost one Misawa machine in a wild fight with enemy fighters.

The pressure of these daily missions to Guadalcanal completely exhausted the land attack crews, and on 24 October they stood down. That night the army launched its greatest bid to retake the island. At one point, in the confusion of battle, it appeared as if the troops had broken through the airfield perimeter, but that report proved erroneous.

An early morning request for an attack on enemy positions on the left bank of the Lunga River brought out 16 *rikko* (nine Kisarazu and seven 753) on the 25th. One from each unit went down in air combat. On the 27th, all of Chitose *Kokutai* redeployed back to Rabaul as reinforcements, but on the last day of the month, the battle-scarred 753 *Ku* Detachment returned to the East Indies with its six remaining aeroplanes.

26 October had seen the great carrier battle of Santa Cruz, from which the Imperial Navy emerged victorious. But with so many veteran aircrew lost in the fight, and with the army's third failure to capture Henderson Field, the triumph at sea rang hollow.

As previously mentioned, on 1 November a redesignation of all navy combat air units took place. Among *rikko* units, all those which had not been redesignated in October now changed their identities as follows:

Mihoro *Kokutai* – 701 *Kokutai*
4th *Kokutai* – 702 *Kokutai*
Chitose *Kokutai* – 703 *Kokutai*
Misawa *Kokutai* – 705 *Kokutai*
Kisarazu *Kokutai* – 707 *Kokutai*
1st *Kokutai* – 752 *Kokutai*
Genzan *Kokutai* – 755 *Kokutai*

In the latter half of October, 751 *Ku* had concentrated its efforts over New Guinea in small night raids over Port Moresby. Troops in Papua, now completely on the defensive, were coming under increasing pressure from advancing Allied forces, and a supply drop on Kokoda by nine Type 1s of 705 *Ku* on 29 October did little to alleviate shortages of every kind.

November opened with yet another night raid on Port Moresby by three land attackers of 751 *Ku*. Nocturnal missions had also been the extent of *rikko* activity over Guadalcanal in the closing days of October, but on 5 November Lt Cdr Gen-ichi Mihara (one of the most revered and senior leaders of the land attack corps, and now the new *hikocho* of 705 *Ku* led 27 *rikko* to Henderson Field. No enemy fighters were encountered, but the AA knocked down a bomber each from 705 and 703 *Ku*.

Five days later ten Type 1s of 707 *Ku* dropped supplies to Japanese troops now starting a desperate defence around Buna, on the north coast of Papua. Twenty-five *rikko* raided Guadalcanal on the 11th, but they lost two each from 703 and 705 *Ku* – three to fighters and one operationally.

On 12 November, under the leadership of Tomo-o Nakamura (now a lieutenant commander), 19 Type 1 *Rikko* (seven 705, nine 703 and three 707) armed with torpedoes went after a major US convoy off Lunga, commanded by their 'old friend' Rear Adm Turner. What followed would break the back of Rabaul's land attack force.

F4Fs of VMF-121 and VMF-112, Army P-39s of the 67th FS and ships' anti-aircraft fire decimated the *rikko* ranks as they went into their low-level runs. The lead formation from 705 lost three bombers, whilst three others (including Nakamura's command aeroplane) made emergency landings at Buin, and one reached Vunakanau. But 705 was lucky compared to 703 and 707. Out of the nine-aeroplane *Chutai* from 703, only one aeroplane made it back. Six went down to enemy fire, and two others (including the leader, Res Lt(jg) Yoshihiko Fukuchi) crash-landed on Guadalcanal, but the men were rescued by Japanese troops on the island and eventually rejoined their unit.

The *shotai* from 707 was wiped out, one *rikko* being destroyed and the remaining two being forced to ditch with nine dead crewmen between them. No fewer than 14 out of the 19 Type 1 *Rikko* sortied had been lost, along with ten entire crews. No torpedoes hit home. Indceed, the damage and casualties aboard the heavy cruiser USS *San Francisco* were caused when it was struck by one of the *rikko* intent on *jibaku* with honour. This was the only wound inflicted on the enemy.

As the only land attack unit in-theatre left with any semblance of fighting efficiency, 751 *Ku* took up the mantle for the rest of November. Following the successful Allied landings near Buna on 16 November, air operations, concentrated for so long over the Solomons, were shifted temporarily again to New Guinea. But on its own, 751 *Ku* could only undertake a series of small night sorties.

703 *Ku*, meanwhile, was removed from the frontline for good on 19 November, departing the Southeastern Area for Japan. Never to fight again, it was disbanded on 15 March 1943.

Disbandment came even more quickly for 707 *Kokutai*. The struggle for Guadalcanal had decimated this most venerable of *rikko* units, and it closed its long, illustrious history on 1 December 1942. Its surviving personnel were absorbed by 705 *Ku*, making the latter a four-*chutai* unit.

1 December brought 701 *Ku* (ex-Mihoro) to Rabaul, still equipped with 36 obsolete Type 96 *Rikko*. Practically all land attack aeroplane operations in December were shouldered by this unit, and these missions were also flown mainly at night, with very occasional assistance from the Type 1s of 751 *Ku*.

By the end of December Japanese troops in New Guinea had met annihilation following a ferocious defence to the last. Small pockets continued to hold out somewhat longer, but all organised resistance would cease in the following days. 31 December was also the day on which Imperial General Headquarters finally swallowed the bitter pill of defeat on Guadalcanal. The decision was finally taken to withdraw Japanese troops from the island, and this was made official in the new year.

BATTLE OF RENNELL ISLAND

As 1943 opened, *rikko* operations in the Southeastern Area were confined increasingly to the hours of darkness, with the three land attack *kokutai* in-theatre – the Type 1-equipped 705 and 751 *Ku*, and the Type 96-equipped 701 *Ku* – continuing their night raids over New Guinea and Guadalcanal during much of January.

On the 17th, however, a rare daylight mission saw 23 aircraft of 705 *Ku* (led by Lt Cdr Mihara) attack Milne Bay, destroying two B-17s, two P-39s, a B-24 and an RAAF Hudson on the ground for no loss.

Then on 29 January a major opportunity presented itself. A search aeroplane spotted a sizeable force of enemy warships near Rennell Island, south of Guadalcanal. With the bitter taste of 8 August and 12 November still fresh, the air staff at Rabaul had finally come to accept that a daylight torpedo attack against well defended American ships would only cause prohibitive losses for little or no result. But the well trained veterans of 701 and 705 *Kokutai* still had one trump card left to play – an aerial torpedo attack at night.

Lt Cdr Nakamura led 16 Type 1s of 705 *Ku*, comprising all the crews in his unit who were proficient in night torpedo attack. A further 15 Type 96s from 701 *Ku* were led by their *hikocho*, Lt Cdr Joji Higai, who together with Gen-ichi Mihara was one of the leading lights of the *rikko* corps. 705 arrived first on the scene.

With the last light of dusk still on the western horizon, Nakamura led his formation around to approach the ships from the south on their starboard quarter, silhouetting them against the horizon as his own aeroplanes remained hidden in the gathering darkness.

At 1919 they went in, pressing home their attack in the fading twilight amid stabbing needles of tracer from the ships, whose proximity-fused shells were being given one of their earliest tests in battle this night. The *rikko* narrowly missed the heavy cruiser USS *Louisville* with one torpedo, while the aeroplane flown by FPO1/c Bunzaburo Imamura fell in flames astern of the heavy cruiser USS *Chicago* for the only loss. 705 *Ku* had taken Rear Adm Robert C Giffen's Task Force 18 by surprise, and had unnerved the American sailors, although no hits had been achieved.

The tropical night came suddenly, but one of the search aeroplanes which had been shadowing the enemy fleet now illuminated the darkness with red and green navigational beacons and a string of parachute flares. At 1940 the Type 96s of 701 *Ku* made their attack, putting two torpedoes into *Chicago's* starboard side. Torpedoes also hit *Louisville* and *Wichita*, but these failed to detonate. 701 lost two aircraft in its attack, but one of them carried Lt Cdr Higai. This was an irreplaceable loss.

Daylight on 30 January found the wounded *Chicago* under tow at four knots. Meanwhile, 751 *Ku* had advanced from Kavieng to Buka the previous day, but the level of skill in this unit was a far cry from what it had been at the beginning of the war, and its men were incapable of joining 705 and 701 *Ku* in a repeat night torpedo attack.

Resigned to heavy casualties in broad daylight, Lt Cdr Nishioka led 11 Type 1s from Buka on the afternoon of the 30th and found *Chicago* north of Rennell Island. As F4Fs from VF-10 rushed to intercept, Nishioka ordered the attack at 1610. Two fell to the fighters before torpedo launch, whilst another caught fire and dropped out of line, although its crew managed to torpedo the destroyer USS *La Vallette* prior to going down. The remaining eight charged on into the murderous fire from the ships.

The *rikko* had released their torpedoes by the time two more were cut down as they hurdled over the cruiser, and four torpedoes struck *Chicago's* damaged starboard side at 1624. The cruiser sank stern-first 20 minutes later. The six G4Ms still flying withdrew at high speed, although two more fell to the F4Fs – of the four survivors, three returned on just one engine. A single *rikko* landed at Munda, on New Georgia, while the other three, including Nishioka, reached Ballale, in the Shortlands.

The Battle of Rennell Island came as a nasty surprise to the US Navy which had no ready counter for aerial torpedo attack at night. For seasoned *rikko* crews of the IJN, night torpedo attack was nothing new, but the early months of victory had provided little incentive to go out and perform such a mission after dark.

At Rennell Island the *rikko* force had demonstrated that it could still startle the foe with its capabilities. But this battle was also the last in which the land attack corps achieved major results at sea. Too many of the IJN's cadre of pre-Pacific War veterans had fallen in battle to be replaced. As the quality of replacement crews declined, and as the Allies grew steadily in strength, the land attack corps found itself increasingly incapable of making a significant impact on the course of events.

Bracketed by flak, *rikko* of 753 *Ku* fly over Darwin during the 2 May 1943 raid. Seven G4Ms and seven escorting 202 *Ku* Zeros suffered damage on this mission, but none were lost. The defending Spitfires suffered no fewer than 14 casualties, however, although only five of these were directly attributable to enemy action (*via Edward M Young*)

Nothing reflected the changed circumstances of Japan's air war, and the shift in doctrine which this imposed, better than the training regimen of 4th *Kokutai* upon its return to Japan in the autumn of 1942. The unit now concentrated on training in twilight and night attack by individual aircraft. Torpedo attacks against shipping was still emphasised, but gone were the majestic 'V of V' formations of 27 aircraft in broad daylight.

In the Southeastern Area, the losses continued. A mere four days after the death in action of Lt Cdr Higai at Rennell Island, Lt Cdr Mihara of 705 *Ku* was lost under tragic circumstances. He fell not to the enemy, but in a mid-air collision with his wingman during a search and attack mission in atrocious weather which claimed no less than six aircraft and most of five complete crews.

Night raids remained the staple for February and March, but a few daylight missions were also flown. Meanwhile, the Type 96 *Rikko*-equipped 701 *Ku*, following steady attrition since December, was disbanded on 15 March, one *buntai* of flight personnel being absorbed into 705 *Ku*.

MORE AUSTRALIAN RAIDS

Outside the Southeastern Area, the pace of war was not nearly so intense. In these regions, *rikko* formations under fighter escort could still perform effective daylight raids without suffering undue losses.

23rd *Koku Sentai* reopened the air campaign over North-western Australia on 15 March 1943 when 19 Type 1 *Rikko* of 753 *Ku* flew a bombing mission against the oil storage tanks at Darwin. The bombers' 26 escorting *Rei-sen* of 202 *Ku* (ex-3rd) tangled with Spitfire VCs of Nos 54 RAF and 457 RAAF Sqns, which only succeeded in damaging eight *rikko*. One Japanese fighter was lost, however, although the *Rei-sen* managed to destroy four Spitfires in return.

Eighteen land attackers returned to the RAAF airfield at Darwin on 2 May, and they managed to drop their bombs before being intercepted. In the combat that ensued during the withdrawal, the escorting 26 Zeros performed excellent work, for no Japanese aircraft were lost. The same could not be said for the Spitfires, which suffered no fewer than 14 losses, of which at least five were directly attributable to the *Rei-sen* of 202 *Ku*.

Exactly one week later seven Type 1s of 753 *Ku* staged through Babo, in Western New Guinea, to hit the remote airfield of Millingimbi, off the coast of Arnhem Land, nearly 450 km east of Darwin. When nine Type 1s returned there on the 28th, they found the airstrip defended by Spitfires of No 457 Sqn. The seven escorting Zeros were unable to protect the bombers and two *rikko* were lost, while a third limped back to base on one engine (a three-hour flight). It was written off in the subsequent crash-landing.

On 28 June nine *rikko* and 27 *Rei-sen* returned to Darwin. One G4M crash-landed at Lautem West, on Timor, during the return flight, while another had its port engine catch fire, but the newly-installed automatic fire-extinguishers worked well, snuffing out the flames.

The steady build up of Allied heavy bombers in the Darwin area was a concern, and on 30 June 23 Type 1s of 753 *Ku* bombed Fenton with excellent results. Despite interception by Spitfires from the time they reached the coast, the land attackers closed ranks and fought their way to the target, while the Zeros of 202 *Ku* provided excellent cover. Four

B-24s and a CW-22 were destroyed on the ground, as well as damage done to equipment and installations. With the exception of one aeroplane written off on landing back at base, the *rikko* suffered no losses.

On 6 July 22 Type 1s went back to Fenton with 26 Zeros, but this mission proved to be a rough one. A running battle with the Spitfires, lasting 40 minutes, ensued, and one *rikko* was shot down and another badly hit. The latter dropped out of formation before the bomb run and eventually crash-landed on Timor. Despite the best efforts of the Spitfires, the bombing was successful, cratering the main runway and torching 27,000 gallons of fuel. One B-24 was destroyed and three others damaged. A second *rikko* was downed during the withdrawal, and the rest brought back five crewmen dead and three wounded, with 13 aircraft damaged.

This mission produced a rare individual citation for bravery, issued to Superior Flight Petty Officer Torao Maruoka, who was the senior navigator/observer in the lead aircraft of the 3rd *Shotai*, 3rd *Chutai* position. With his *rikko* badly hit by the Spitfires, his pilot dead and co-pilot seriously wounded, Maruoka took over the controls and managed to fly the aeroplane back to base for a safe landing.

The 6 July mission was the last daylight raid flown over the Darwin area, although night sorties continued for another four months. The last raid occurred on the night of 11/12 November, 753 *Ku* losing one aeroplane on that mission – the *rikko* flown by the newly-arrived *hikocho*, Cdr Michio Horii, as well as *buntaicho* Lt Takeharu Fujiwara. The loss of two senior officers in one blow had a massive impact on the unit's operations, and further missions over Darwin were immediately cancelled.

Thereafter, as the Allied counteroffensive gained momentum, the demands of other theatres eventually stripped the East Indies of *rikko* units. Prior to that, however, one more mission flown by the land attackers in this region is worthy of mention.

In November 1943, the battle-scarred 705 *Kokutai* arrived at Padang, on the south coast of Sumatra, for rest and reformation following combat over New Guinea and the Solomons. After a period of recuperation, it took over patrol functions from 753 *Ku*. The latter unit, having served for so long in this theatre, was in turn called away to the Central Pacific between November 1943 and January 1944.

In December 1943, 705 *Ku* took part in an operation long in the planning – a bombing mission over India. Nine Type 1s moved up to Toungoo, in Burma, and on 5 December, after rendezvousing with an escort of 27 Zeros from 331 *Ku* over Magwe, they headed for Calcutta. The *rikko* formed the second wave of an attack which followed the Japanese Army's 7th *Hikodan* (Flying Brigade). All aircraft returned safely following the successful bombing of the Kittapore Docks in the navy's single contribution to air operations in a theatre dominated by the JAAF.

But in February 1944 705 *Ku* also left the region and transferred to Peleliu to face the American onslaught once more. This left just 732 *Ku* in the South-western Area, the *kokutai* serving as an operational training unit for *rikko* crews. It had formed at Toyohashi, in Japan, on 1 October 1943, and had been based at Ayer Tawar, in Malaya, from December that year. The unit undertook anti-submarine patrols in the region, but left for Digos, in the Philippines, in April 1944 to serve in the frontline against invading American forces.

OPERATION *I-GO*

The growing strength of Allied forces in the Southeastern Area was ominous in its implications. Adm Isoroku Yamamoto, Commander in Chief Combined Fleet, decided to commit, on a temporary basis, the full weight of the navy's carrier-based units to the task of dealing decisively with this threat, and he ordered them to land bases at Rabaul and Kavieng. Operating from these airfields, they were to fly alongside land-based air units in a series of major strikes against enemy air forces and shipping throughout the region.

Known as Operation *I-Go*, this major deployment of air units was personally commanded by Yamamoto himself, who flew down to Rabaul with his Combined Fleet Staff on 3 April 1943. The majority of sorties flown during this operation were by fighters and single-engined bombers, but the land attackers took part on two occasions.

Firstly, on 12 April, 751 *Ku Hikocho* Lt Cdr Masaichi Suzuki led 17 Type 1s from 751 and 27 from 705 (escorted by no less than 131 *Rei-sen*) against the Port Moresby airfields. Bombing from a height of 8000 metres, they inflicted serious damage, destroying a Beaufighter and three B-25s, as well as damaging 15 other aircraft, cratering the runways and setting fire to a fuel dump. But losses to intercepting P-38s were also heavy.

751 *Ku*, in the lead, took the brunt of the combat, losing six to the Lightnings, while a seventh machine was written off in a crash-landing at Lae. The following 705 *Ku* formation, led by Tomo-o Nakamura, suffered 11 aircraft damaged, but limited its losses to one aeroplane destroyed in a landing at Lae.

On the 14th, Lt Cdr Shichiso Miyauchi – veteran leader of the attack on *Prince of Wales* and *Repulse*, and newly-arrived replacement *hikocho* for 705 *Ku* – led 26 *rikko* of 705 and 17 of 751 to Milne Bay. En route, no less than six aircraft from 751 dropped out, including two involved in a mid-air collision, leaving only 11 participants from that unit. During air combat with American P-38s and RAAF Kittyhawks over the target, 705 *Ku* lost three aircraft outright and a fourth in a crash-landing at Gasmata, New Britain, while 751 *Ku* also had one aeroplane forced down at the latter site. At least two of the *rikko* had been victims of 1Lt Richard I Bong of the 9th FS/49th FG (see *Aircraft of the Aces 14 - P-38 Lightning Aces of the Pacific and CBI* for further details).

Misled by exaggerated reports of success by returning aircrew, Adm

This early post-war memorial was set up by returning Japanese veterans on Bougainville next to the crash site of Adm Yamamoto's *rikko*. The aircraft's tail number 323 was still clearly evident when this photograph was taken, although the G4M was later vandalised and the tail numbers removed (*Second Yamamoto Mission Association via J F Lansdale*)

Yamamoto decided that the object of Operation *I-Go* had been achieved, and he declared the operation concluded on 16 April. Some telling blows had indeed been struck, but the overall level of damage inflicted on the allies was much lower than perceived, and entirely inadequate to blunt Allied strength in the region.

On 18 April Adm Yamamoto and members of his staff boarded two Type 1 *Rikko* of 705 *Ku* at Lakunai (East Field), Rabaul, and set out on an inspection tour of frontline bases. The aircraft headed for Ballale, the tiny island base in the Shortlands off Bougainville's southern tip, but they were destined never to arrive.

As is well known, the *rikko* were ambushed by P-38s from Guadalcanal in an operation made possible by American codebreakers. Yamamoto died in the jungle crash of Aircraft No 323, commanded and flown by veteran pilot FCPO Takashi Kotani, near Moila Point on southern Bougainville. The other aircraft, No 326, commanded by FPO1/c Hiroaki Tanimura and piloted by FPO2/c Hiroshi Hayashi, managed to crash in the waters offshore. Vice Adm Matome Ugaki, Yamamoto's Chief of Staff and two others, including pilot Hayashi, were the only survivors.

One of Japan's ablest and most air-minded admirals, and one who had helped to give birth to the *rikujo kogeki-ki*, had died in just such an aircraft in a theatre already strewn with the charred and twisted wreckage of many of its sisters.

For 705 *Kokutai*, that was not the end of its losses for the day. That night, ten Type 1s sortied from Buka on a mission to Guadalcanal and, in the early hours of the 19th, lost the aircraft of FCPO Sadao Furuya over the target. He fell to the guns of a P-70 nightfighter of the 6th Night Fighter Squadron, flown by Capt Earl C Bennett. Furuya had gained the dubious distinction of becoming the first nightfighter victory of the USAAF. The cloak of night was no longer a safe haven for the *Rikko*.

CENTRAL SOLOMONS

The month of May saw the return of 25th *Koku Sentai* to the Southeastern Area for a second tour of duty in the region with its component units, 702 *Ku* (ex-4th *Ku*) and 251 *Ku* (ex-Tainan *Ku*). 702 had 47 Type 1 *rikko*

Aircraft of 4th *Chutai*, 705 *Kokutai* take off from Tinian in mid-May, 1943 to return to the fray at Rabaul. Only individual aircraft numbers are carried on the tail, units active in the Southeastern Area having painted out the unit code on their aircraft from as early as September 1942. Compared to the old Misawa *Ku* days, the *chutai* stripes used by 705 *Ku* were now much thinner. All aircraft in the photo carry the fuselage *hinomaru* in a white square, which was a style most prevalent during the first half of 1943 (*via* S Nohara)

in place at Vunakanau (West Field), Rabaul, by 14 May, and had flown its first mission in-theatre the previous night when six bombers struck targets on Guadalcanal. The 14th also saw the return to Rabaul of 705 *Ku*, which had been on Tinian since 27 April, undertaking a spell of training and rest.

With these units back at Rabaul, 751 *Ku* was in turn scheduled for a period of well earned rest on Tinian. Before that, however, the unit was to fly one more mission. On 14 May Lt Cdr Nishioka led 18 *rikko*, under escort from 33 *Rei-sen* of 251 *Ku*, on a daylight raid on Oro Bay The IJN force was intercepted en route by P-38s and P-40s of the 49th FG, and a total of six land attackers went down, including three that ditched – one of the latter carried Nishioka. Japanese submarines later rescued two of the downed crews, but the veteran *hikotaicho* was not among them. 751 *Ku* flew to Tinian as scheduled three days later, but without their respected flight leader.

Following months of heavy action, and serious losses in combat, the *rikko* corps was confronted with a chronic shortage of personnel by mid-1943. And this situation had arisen despite the formation on 1 April of a

Model 11s of 3rd *Chutai*, 705 *Kokutai* fly over Simpson Harbour, Rabaul, in mid-1943. Note the truncated tail cone on aircraft No 360, in the foreground. This modification was introduced in the spring of 1943 to improve the field of fire for the 20 mm tail cannon. The narrow slit opening in the original tail cone allowed gun traverse in one plane only, the gunner being required to rotate the cone in order to direct the gun in a different plane. 705 *Ku* originally had three *chutai*, but both the *chutai* stripe system and the number block assignments were changed following the incorporation of disbanded ex-707 *Ku* personnel as a fourth *chutai* in December 1942 (*Fujiro Hino via Koku Fan via Dr Yashuo Izawa via Larry Hickey*)

Aircraft No 336 of 705 *Ku* crash-landed at Bugmar Beach, on New Georgia, following the disastrous torpedo strike against Allied shipping on 30 June 1943. 705 lost four other *rikko* and their crews on this mission, out of the nine despatched. 702 *Ku* lost 13 crews and 14 aircraft out of 17 (*Al Simmons Collection via Larry Hickey*)

This photograph shows the port side *rikko* No 336. The bomber was commanded by Sup FPO Shuji Sakurai on the 30 June mission that saw it so badly shot up. Following the addition of a fourth *chutai* to 705 *Ku*, the horizontal tail stripe (clearly visible on this machine) is believed to have denoted 3rd *Chutai* rather than the 2nd, as was the case with the unit's old three *chutai* structure. In this particular instance, however, the individual aircraft number continues to reflect a 2nd *Chutai* machine (*via Robert C Mikesh*)

This formation flight of 705 *Ku* Model 11s was photographed during the Central Solomons campaign. Note the extreme weathering and unpainted replacement panels on the nearest aircraft – vivid evidence of the heavy combat in this theatre (*via Robert C Mikesh*)

new *rikko* operational training unit, Toyohashi *Kokutai*. As it absorbed replacements and began training on Tinian, 751 *Ku* was forced to reorganise crew assignments, reducing the standard complement per aeroplane from seven to five, including dispensing with co-pilots. This became the norm in other *rikko* units as well.

Most of June was spent on night missions and patrol flights, and losses also began to crop up on these latter missions as well, due primarily to enemy bombers flying similar sorties. With their unprotected fuel tanks, the *rikko* almost always lost out in these lonely duels over the Pacific.

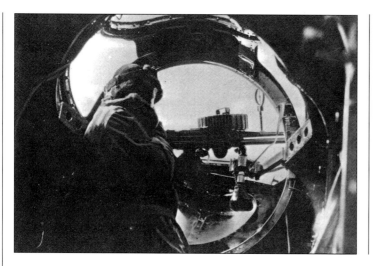

A gunner at his 7.7mm Type 92 MG in the dorsal blister position of the Model 11 in the summer of 1943 over the Solomon Islands. The rear half of the blister covering can be seen stowed in front of the gunner, beneath the machine gun. The Type 92 weapon differed little from the World War 1-vintage British Lewis machine gun from which it was derived, and was wholly inadequate as defensive armament in the hostile skies of 1943 (*via Edward M Young*)

The Allies made their next major move on the last day of the month, with simultaneous landings on Rendova, in the Central Solomons, and Nassau Bay, in New Guinea. With the Japanese Army taking increasing responsibility for air operations in this theatre, navy air units focused their reaction against Rendova.

Confronting a new enemy landing, the air command felt compelled to strike back at the earliest opportunity by whatever means possible. Once again, the *rikko* crews were ordered out on a daylight torpedo mission, and it is a tribute to their stoic bravery that the attack was pressed home – 17 Type 1s of 702 *Ku* and nine from 705 were led by the 702 *Ku Hikotaicho*, Lt Cdr Genzo Nakamura. Precious minutes lost in a search for the ships, which were eventually found in Blanche Channel, between Rendova and New Georgia, brought a swarm of F4Us and F4Fs.

Three *rikko* from 702, including Nakamura, managed to return, whilst a fourth aircraft ditched and the crew was saved. Thirteen others never came back. 705 *Ku* counted four missing and one crash-landed. In all, 19 out of 26 aircraft, and 17 crews, were lost. About ten *rikko* fought their way through the fighters and flak to launch torpedoes, but their only score was a single torpedo hit against the transport USS *McCawley*, flagship of their old nemesis Kelly Turner.

To fill the gap left by such losses, 1st *Chutai* of 751 *Ku* with 12 *rikko*, led by Lt Masao Motozu, was ordered down to Rabaul on 1 July. Two *Chutai* of 752 *Kokutai*, led by the colourful Lt Goro Nonaka, were also rushed to Vunakanau on detached duty – 21 Type 1s were flown in from the far north on 9 July.

Formerly the 1st *Kokutai*, 752 *Ku* had returned to Kisarazu, Japan, from the Central Pacific at the end of 1942, changing places with 755 *Ku*

Trailing a stream of vapour in the humid air, a fully bombed-up Z2-310 of 1st *Chutai*, 751 *Kokutai* is seen outbound on a mission during the Central Solomons campaign. Led by Lt Masao Motozu, this *chutai* saw combat on detached service at Rabaul during the first half of July 1943, suffering crippling losses over New Georgia. The aircraft in the foreground clearly shows the yellow wing leading edge identification stripe, which was first introduced in the autumn of 1942 (*via S Nohara*)

(ex-Genzan). During the opening months of 1943, 752 *Ku* converted from Type 96 to Type 1 *Rikko*, and in the wake of the American landings on Japanese-held Attu, in the Aleutian Islands, on 11 May 1943, a detachment flew to Paramushiro, in the Kuriles, to lend what support it could. However, the perennial fog in this sub-arctic region made air operations extremely difficult.

On 22 May, 19 torpedo-armed *rikko* led by Lt Nonaka managed to attack the destroyer USS *Phelps* and the cruiser USS *Charleston* off Attu, then dropped supplies to the garrison and returned with only one loss due to weather. In spite of optimistic claims by the crews involved, they had achieved no hits.

The next day Nonaka led 17

The waist gunner of a 4th *Chutai*, 705 *Kokutai* G4M looks out over a formation of *rikko* from his port blister. This photograph was taken in the Central Solomons in the summer of 1943 (*Author's Collection*)

Type 1s to Attu in an attempt to bomb enemy troop positions, but clouds obscured the target and they were forced to shed their bombs when attacked by P-38s. In the last aerial engagement of the Aleutians campaign, the unescorted *rikko* lost two of their number shot down during a running battle that lasted a full 30 minutes. A third bomber ditched, and most of the crew was saved. In return they managed to bring down two of the Lightnings with their 20 mm tail cannon. That was the extent of *rikko* combat in the far north, and the Attu garrison died to a man in a final suicide charge on 29 May.

Further south, in the sweltering heat of the Central Solomons, daylight raids continued into July as the enemy made landings on New Georgia. A six aeroplane raid on Rovianna Lagoon cost 705 *Ku* two *rikko* and one crew in air combat on the 7th, while another was lost on a mission to Enogai, north of Munda, four days later.

Losses on the 15th were particularly heavy when 751 *Ku* Detachment had no fewer than six aircraft shot down in a 40-minute battle with F4Us, F4Fs and P-40s during a mission to Rovianna. One of those to die during this disastrous engagement was the detachment leader, Lt Motozu. Five days later, 751 *Ku Chutai* returned to its parent unit on Tinian with its three surviving *rikko*.

The losses of 15 July put an end to daylight missions for the *rikko*, but night sorties continued throughout the region. On the night of 14/15 August, single *rikko* from 705 and 752 *Ku* fell to nightflying P-38s over the Guadalcanal area. The following night, nine 702 *Ku* aircraft with bombs and seven torpedo-armed *rikko* of 752 *Ku* attacked shipping off Gatukai Island. The only casualty on this occasion was a 752 machine damaged in a landing mishap.

At the beginning of September the 752 *Ku* Detachment rejoined its parent unit in Japan, although the majority of its crews were transferred into 702 *Ku* and remained on operations at Rabaul until mid-October.

705 *Ku* withdrew to Tinian for rest and replenishment on 5 September, while all of 751 *Ku*, now rested and brought up to strength, advanced to Rabaul during the first week of the month. 705 was destined never to return to Rabaul, transferring subsequently to the East Indies.

A new series of daylight missions were carried out in September as Allied landings took place around Lae, New Guinea. On the 4th, 702 *Ku* sent 12 aeroplanes to attack shipping in the area, losing three shot down, while the leader made a forced landing at Cape Gloucester on the south-western tip of New Britain.

The next day eight *rikko* of 751 *Ku* managed to bomb vessels off Hopoi, east of Lae, without loss. A similar raid flown on the 6th by 17 aeroplanes of 751 *Ku*, in conjunction with fighters and dive-bombers, resulted in two *rikko* being lost and two damaged.

On 22 September an enemy landing at Finschhafen threatened to cut New Guinea off from New Britain

by bringing the Dampier and Vitiaz Straits under Allied control. IJN HQ on Rabaul decided there was no choice but to send the *rikko* out on a daylight torpedo attack, although everyone knew this would be a virtual suicide mission. Of the eight bombers sortied by 751 *Ku*, aeroplane No 324, flown by FCPO Jitsuyoshi Kuramasu, was the only one to return. Another managed to reach Cape Gloucester, where it was written off in a crash-landing. The *rikko* had scored no hits.

Top and above
In October 1943 Rabaul itself came under attack from bombers of the US Fifth Air Force. Taken on the 24th of the month from a low-flying B-25 of the 345th Bomb Group (BG), these shots show Model 11s of the 3rd *Chutai*, 702 *Kokutai* caught in the open in their dispersal area at West Field (Vunakanau)
(*both John C Hanna Collection via Larry Hickey*)

Heavily weathered *rikko* No 320 of the 2nd *Chutai*, 702 *Kokutai* was photographed in its revetment during the 24 October raid
(*Victor W Tatelman Collection via Larry Hickey*)

Aircraft No 321 of 2nd *Chutai*, 702 *Ku* reveals parafrag damage to its tail sustained during the 24 October raid (*Victor W Tatelman Collection via Larry Hickey*)

An earlier photograph of a then undamaged No 321, taken during the 12 October 1943 raid. This aircraft was crewed by Lt(jg) Hidezumi Maruyama as pilot and FCPO Seiji Sekine as senior observer/navigator. On the night of 12/13 November 1943, this crew torpedoed the light cruiser USS *Denver* off Bougainville and returned to base despite taking 380 hits. This incident was immortalised in Sekine's classic account of *rikko* combat over New Guinea and the Solomons, *Hono-o no Tsubasa* (*Wings Of Flame*). The aircraft carries the late production Model 11 tail gun position more commonly associated with the G4M2. However, the bulge above the covered engine nacelles indicate that the aeroplane still had the older exhaust stacks fitted with flame dampeners, rather than the later individual exhaust stacks (*Larry Tanberg Collection via Larry Hickey*)

OPERATION *RO-GO*

The weight of Allied raids forced the Japanese to abandon their base at Buin, in southern Bougainville, in late October. And from the 12th of that month Rabaul itself came under daylight air attack from the US Fifth Air Force, which was joined by US carrier forces the following month.

Adm Mineichi Koga, Yamamoto's successor as C-in-C Combined Fleet, launched Operation *Ro-Go*, a repeat of the *I-Go* Operation conducted by his predecessor. Again, he hoped to redress the balance in-theatre with another temporary deployment of carrier units to Rabaul and Kavieng. But on the very day of their arrival (1 November), American forces landed at Cape Torokina, on Bougainville, and *Ro-Go* became merely a series of raids flown against the Torokina beachhead in which the Japanese suffered huge losses for little gain.

The land attack aeroplanes of 702 and 751 *Ku* fought on, conducting a series of night torpedo attacks against American warships in the waters around Bougainville, starting on 8 November. That night, a *rikko* managed to put a torpedo into the light cruiser USS *Birmingham*, but the two land attack *kokutai* lost seven aeroplanes in the effort.

As crew inexperience and the chaos and confusion of explosions in the night conspired against the Japanese, a pattern was set which would continue for the rest of the war. Huge claims were being made against

This well-known photograph shows aircraft No 350 of the 3rd *Chutai*, 702 *Kokutai* under parafrag attack during the 12 October raid. This was the first low-level strike flown in the October/November 1943 series of attacks on Rabaul by the Fifth Air Force, and the first time base personnel at Rabaul had seen parafrags. At first they thought they were under attack by paratroopers (*John C Hanna Collection via Larry Hickey*)

Published here for the first time is this shot of the same aircraft, but from the port side. No 350 was one of the older aircraft in 702 *Ku*, as shown by the extreme weathering of its finish – more evident here on the port side of the aircraft. The white square fuselage *hinomaru* was quite a rare marking by this late date (*Larry Tanberg Collection via Larry Hickey*)

minimal results. Five aeroplanes of 702 *Ku* gained no hits on 11/12 November, but on the following night the aeroplane flown by Lt(jg) Hidezumi Maruyama (No 321) of 702 *Ku* put a torpedo into the light cruiser USS *Denver*. The *rikko* was badly shot up in the process, being holed no less than 380 times in the wings and fuselage. Despite this damage, the G4M was successfully flown back to base, where the aeroplane was deemed to be beyond repair and was duly scrapped.

On the night of 16/17 November, SFPO Gintaro Kobayashi of 702 *Ku* sank the destroyer-transport USS *McKean* with a torpedo. His starboard engine caught fire just as he made his run, but he managed to extinguish the flames with an adroit side-slipping manoeuvre and return to base on one engine. But alas, isolated feats of arms such as this were not enough to stop the momentum of the Allied counter-offensive.

This series of Fifth Air Force photos provides a near-complete record of the *rikko* flown by 3rd *Chutai*, 702 *Kokutai* in October 1943. Seen here is aircraft No 358 (*Larry Tanberg Collection via Larry Hickey*)

This 4th *Chutai*, 702 *Kokutai* aircraft was also photographed in its dispersal during the 24 October raid. Note the distinctive thin and thick stripes on the rudder only (*Thomas D Riggs Collection via Larry Hickey*)

Aircraft No 324 of 751 *Ku*, flown by FCPO Jitsuyoshi Kuramasu, is seen at West Field, Rabaul, on 24 October. Kuramasu and his crew, flying in their previous aircraft (also numbered 324), were the only ones to return to Rabaul following the suicidal daylight torpedo mission off Finschhafen on 22 September 1943 (*Thomas D Riggs Collection via Larry Hickey*)

Another photograph of 751 *Ku* aircraft at Rabaul in October 1943. Aircraft No 373 still carries the unit designator '51' on its tail. Note also the refuelling bowser caught out in the open by the low-level B-25 raid (*Victor W Tatelman Collection via Larry Hickey*)

On 1 December 702 *Kokutai* was disbanded, with most surviving personnel either returning to Japan or joining 751 *Ku*, which was now the sole *rikko* unit remaining at Rabaul.

751 *Ku* had been selected to be the first unit to receive the new power turret-equipped Model 22 Type 1 *Rikko*, and at the beginning of December some 751 personnel, including FCPO Kuramasu, were sent to Japan to receive the first three. However, they soon discovered that the new model was still fraught with problems, despite having entered production in July. With the aeroplane still being tested by the Air Technical Arsenal as 1943 drew to a close, plans for 751's conversion were abandoned, and personnel returned to Rabaul with now clearly obsolescent Model 11s.

751 *Kokutai* continued to fight on in the face of overwhelming opposition, the Allies steadily closing the ring around Rabaul. Finally, in the wake of the devastating raid by US carrier forces against Truk, in the Caroline Islands, on 17-18 February 1944, the Japanese were forced to pull all air units out of Rabaul. By the 20th, 751 *Ku* had withdrawn its remaining 15 aircraft to Truk.

CENTRAL PACIFIC

Following the return to Japan of 752 *Kokutai* in December 1942, *rikko* operations in the Central Pacific were left solely in the hands of 755 *Ku* (ex-Genzan). The last of the land attack units to give up its Type 96 *Rikko*, 755 had just begun to convert to the Type 1 when the relative quiet of this vast, island-studded theatre was shattered on 1 September 1943. A US

Photographed at East Field (Lakunai), Rabaul, during the 2 November 1943 strike by Fifth Air Force aircraft, this Type 1 *Rikko* Model 11 was being used in the transport role. It is parked next to an A6M3 Model 22 *Rei-sen* with its wingtips folded, the fighter almost certainly hailing from 204 *Ku*. The fact that the Type 1 is a *rikko* (G4M1) rather than a Type 1 Land-based Transport (G6M1-L) is evident by the circular rear fuselage hatch in the *hinomaru*, as opposed to the oval access door of the transport version. The tail code '731-01' shows it to be a machine of 11th Air Fleet HQ Transport Unit. Note the steel matting on the ground next to the *Rei-sen (John C Hanna Collection via Larry Hickey)*

Published here for the first time is a full photo of the tail markings of 1001 *Kokutai,* which was the first specialised transport and ferrying unit formed within the IJN. It appears on the rear fuselage wreck of a Type 1 Land-based Transport photographed from the air during a raid on Kavieng, New Ireland, in February 1944. The *katakana* letter 'Yo' (appearing like a backward 'E') followed by 'A' indicates the first unit assigned to Yokosuka Naval District following Yokosuka *Kokutai* itself, which simply used the *katakana* letter 'Yo' as its code. The high individual aircraft number 987 (900s range indicating transport) and double tail stripe, signifying *chutai* affiliation, are also interesting features (*Fred Robinson Jr Collection via Larry Hickey*)

task force centred around a new generation of aircraft carriers, and embarking the new Grumman F6F Hellcat fighter, struck Marcus Island.

On 19 September the enemy's fast carriers attacked targets in the Gilbert Islands. Wake Island was next, struck on 6-7 October – US forces, operating out of Pearl Harbor on the other side of the International Dateline, recorded dates one day previous in the early part of the Central Pacific Campaign.

Practically all Japanese aircraft on the island, including 23 *rikko*, were destroyed or severely damaged. Then, as quickly as they had come, the enemy carriers departed the area. But this proved merely a lull in the typhoon. The long-dreaded US offensive in the Central Pacific was about to begin.

THE GILBERTS

Completing its conversion to Type 1 *Rikko* during October, 755 *Ku* concentrated its remaining forces on Roi, in Kwajalein Atoll. On 21 November enemy troops stormed ashore on Makin and Tarawa, in the Gilbert Islands, and for the rest of the month, repeated night torpedo attacks were pressed home against the US fleet by aircraft of 755 *Ku* and 752 *Ku* – the latter unit had been called in as reinforcement. On the evening of the invasion they damaged the light carrier USS *Independence* with a torpedo hit, but that was the extent of their success. All organised resistance had ended on the two islands by the 25th.

The US carriers next hit Roi and Wotje in the Marshalls on 5 December. That night, nine aeroplanes of 752 sortied from Maloelap under the leadership of Lt Cdr Nonaka, the *rikko* striking the task force at much the same time as eight Type 1s from 753 *Ku* Advance Echelon, which had just arrived at Roi that afternoon after departing Java on 30 November. Although the force lost two 753 aircraft in action, the *rikko* scored one hit on the newly-commissioned USS *Lexington*, causing extensive damage. The bomber crews, and particularly Nonaka's men of 752 *Ku*, were becoming extremely proficient in these night torpedo attacks. And it was only a lack of numbers that prevented the land attackers from having a greater impact.

On 7 December, with 753 *Ku* Advance Echelon having arrived, and with 752 *Ku* already in-theatre, the greatly depleted 755 *Ku* withdrew to Tinian in order to rebuild its strength.

THE MARSHALLS

24 January 1944 saw the arrival at Tinian of the main body of 753 *Ku* fresh from Kendari, in the Celebes. This was none too soon, for on the 30th (29th by the American calendar) Roi, the focal point of Japanese air

Groundcrew manhandle a torpedo into position beneath a late production Model 11, probably of 752 *Kokutai*, in December 1943. Close examination of the cowl flap details of this well-known photograph reveals that the aircraft's engines boast individual exhaust stacks, indicating a late production machine. For much of the Pacific War, the standard IJN aerial torpedo was the Type 91, a weapon which was greatly modified and improved over time. Both the basic Type 91 and the Type 91 *Kai* 1 weighed 784 kg and had warheads weighing 149.5 kg. The Type 91 *Kai* 2, modified for running in shallow depths, had a larger warhead of 204 kg and weighed 838 kg in total. The ultimate Type 91 was the *Kai* 7, with a warhead of 420 kg – more than twice that of the *Kai* 2 – and a total weight of 1060 kg. While all other versions could be carried by carrier-based attack aeroplanes as well as by *rikko*, the *Kai* 7 was exclusively for use by the G4M (*via Edward M Young*)

strength in the Marshalls, was hit by a major US carrier strike. In addition to eight *rikko* destroyed on the ground, 752 *Ku* lost six in the air to F6Fs of VF-6, half of them to Lt(jg) Alex Vraciu (see *Aircraft of the Aces 10 - Hellcat Aces of World War 2* for further details).

The enemy came ashore at Roi on 2 February, and in the ground fighting which followed, headquarters staff of 24th *Koku Sentai*, along with elements of 752 and 753 *Ku* who were there, were annihilated. Among those to fall was Lt Cdr Miyoshi Nabeta, a veteran of Malaya and Guadalcanal, who had been posted in as a staff officer to 24th *Koku*

Above left
A late-production Model 11 of 755 *Kokutai* overflies the Marshall Islands in November 1943. The wartime censor has blanked out the tail markings on this aircraft, but the white stripe along the trailing edge of the rudder had signified a *shotai* leader in this unit ever since its Type 96 *Rikko* days as Genzan *Kokutai*. The double rear fuselage stripe (note it does not completely surround the fuselage) also dates back to Type 96 days, and is a hangover from the unit's period with 2nd *Rengo Kokutai* (Combined *Kokutai*), later redesignated 22nd *Koku Sentai* (*Author's Collection*)

These late production Model 11s of 3rd *Chutai*, 752 *Kokutai* were destroyed at Roi, on Kwajalein Atoll in the Marshall Islands, during the US carrier strikes of January/February 1944. 752 *Ku* was very active in night torpedo attacks against American warships during the Gilberts and Marshalls campaigns from November 1943 through to February 1944 (*USAAF via James F Lansdale*)

Sentai the previous year. 18 February saw the Americans land on Eniwetok, but by then the Japanese could offer little resistance in the air following major losses to enemy carrier aeroplanes at Truk. Three days later 752 *Ku* was sent back to Japan to rebuild itself at Toyohashi.

TRUK AND THE MARIANAS

As the the main anchorage of the Combined Fleet in the Central Pacific, Truk, in the Caroline Islands, was an important target for the US Navy, and on 17-18 February it was struck by carrier aircraft in their most devastating attack to date.

Just a week prior to the raid the main elements of the Combined Fleet had departed Truk for safer havens further west, but the naval aircraft nevertheless sank over 40 vessels still moored in the lagoon, and destroyed 300+ aircraft. Amid the carnage, the land attackers managed one counter-attack on the night of the 17/18th, in which a 755 *Ku rikko* flying from Tinian torpedoed USS *Intrepid*, putting that carrier out of action for several months.

The effects of the Truk raid were felt far and wide. Units which had continued to hold out against tremendous odds at Rabaul were now pulled back to cover the horrendous losses, finally bringing an end to Japanese air activity in the Southeastern Area. It also compelled the high command to deploy elements of 1st Air Fleet to the Marianas before their training was complete.

Those units sent into action were essentially a collection of newly-established land-based *kokutai* drawn from 1st Air Fleet's second formation, which was originally formed as a mobile reserve to be used in a decisive battle with the enemy. The one *rikko* unit initially formed under 1st Air Fleet control was 761 *Kokutai*, which was also known as the 'Ryu' *Butai*, or 'Dragon' Unit. Established on 1 July 1943, 761 *Kokutai* began its training at Kanoya, and was given priority in the assignment of new Type 1 Model 22 aircraft following the abortive attempt to equip 751 *Ku* at Rabaul with this model.

In the immediate aftermath of the raid on Truk, an advance echelon of 1st Air Fleet units deployed to Central Pacific bases, and by 22 February 761 *Ku* had 24 new Type 1s at Tinian. On that day a patrolling *rikko* found the US carriers on the prowl once more, and during the course of the evening, and the following morning, 761 *Ku* expended all 24 aeroplanes on strength without achieving any notable success. The carriers struck the Marianas on the morning of the 23rd, concentrating on Saipan

This Model 11 of 761 *Kokutai* was photographed during the unit's training phase in Japan in 1943. The *kanji* character *'Ryu'* (Dragon) on the bomber's tail reflected the unit's name (*via S Nohara*)

and Tinian. In its wake, the advance echelon of 1st Air Fleet was practically wiped out.

TOKUSETSU HIKOTAI

With Japan retreating throughout the Pacific, and its forward bases increasingly isolated as the Allies consolidated their command of the air and sea, Imperial Navy air units were now confronted with a shortage of skilled mechanics. Airmen could fly from one base to another, but experienced groundcrew often found themselves stranded on island bases.

Thus, on 4 March 1944, in order to provide greater flexibility for its air operations, the IJN instituted a fundamental restructuring of its *kokutai*. The flying echelons (*hikotai*) of the *kokutai* were spun off as independent units, known as *tokusetsu hikotai* (special establishment *hikotai*), with their own numerical designations, while the *kokutai* essentially became ground-based service organisations. This, in theory, would allow *hikotai* to deploy freely from one base to another as the situation demanded, operating under assignment to whatever *kokutai* was most appropriate at any given time.

The new system was not imposed at once throughout the naval air service, but in stages as the need arose. Under the new system, on 4 March 1944, the flying echelon personnel of 755 and 751 *Ku* were split up, half forming Attack (*Kogeki*) *Hikotai* 701 (K701) and assigned back to 755 *Ku*, while the remainder formed Attack *Hikotai* 704 (K704), assigned to 751 *Ku*.

705 *Kokutai* ceased to operate land-based attack aircraft at this time, its *rikko* personnel being formed into Attack *Hikotai* 706 (K706) and assigned to 755 *Ku*. Thus, 755 *Kokutai* was now composed of two *hikotai*, K701 and K706, while 751 *Ku* operated K704. These *hikotai* were all given a standard complement of 36 aeroplanes, plus 12 reserve, but actual strength often fell considerably short of this figure.

PALAU AND WESTERN NEW GUINEA

During March, 1st Air Fleet and other units mauled by the recent US carrier raids painstakingly rebuilt themselves. A successful long-range attack out of Truk was conducted without loss by K706 against Eniwetok Atoll on the night of 9 March, but such actions proved to be exceptional.

During the month, land attack units began to fall back on Peleliu, in the Palau Islands, and by late March elements of 761 and 751 *Ku* were largely based there, while 755 *Ku* had aeroplanes in the Marianas and at Truk. In addition, Yokosuka *Kokutai*, now deploying combat detach-

This veteran Model 11 was still being operated by 732 *Kokutai* at Ayer Tawar, in Malaya, during the spring of 1944. Note the Army Type 1 Fighters (Ki-43 *Hayabusa*) in the background. 732 *Ku* was operating in the operational training role at the time this photograph was taken. Later equipped with Model 22s, it took part in combat over western New Guinea (*via Bunrindo K K*)

'Graveyard of the Dragons'. These three shots were taken by a Marine Corps photographer following the invasion of Peleliu, in the Palau Islands. All Model 22s of 761 *Kokutai*, they were destroyed in March and April 1944. Aircraft No 76 was handed down from the Yokosuka *Ku* detachment following the latter's departure from the area in mid-July, as is evidenced by the overpainting of its tail code. Some aircraft, such as No 41, still carry the *kanji* marking on the tail (*USMC*)

ments in addition to continuing in its role as the navy's operational test centre, had 18 Type 1 Model 22s on Tinian by 28 March. The detachment remained in-theatre until 14 April, at which time it returned to Japan, leaving its remaining aircraft behind in the Marianas for other units such as 761 *Ku*.

US carriers now attacked the Palau Islands on 30-31 March. Starting on the night of 29 March, the land attackers of 761, 751, 755 and Yoko-suka *Ku* attempted to take on the enemy task force from their bases on Peleliu, Tinian and Guam, but once again no results were achieved, and the scale of loss in ships and aircraft proved second only to the Truk raid.

1 April 1944 saw the formation of three more independent *hikotai*, when the flying echelon of 752 *Kokutai* became K703, 753 *Ku* became K705 and Toyohashi *Kokutai*, which had become a combat unit and been

'One shot lighter'. Aircraft No 72 (a Model 22 of 761 *Ku*) erupts in flames over the Central Pacific on 26 May 1944, having been attacked not by an American fighter or even a patrol bomber, but by a PB2Y Coronado flying boat of VP-13. This is graphic proof of the stark vulnerability of the Type 1 *Rikko*, as well as the complete reversal of fortunes suffered by Japanese air forces in 1944 (*National Archives*)

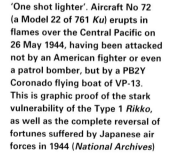

No 26 (a Model 22 of 761 *Kokutai*) is seen under attack at Jefman/ Samate (Sorong), in western New Guinea, on 16 June 1944. By this time most aircraft in 761 *Ku* had had the 'Dragon' *kanji* character painted out, leaving just the two-digit individual aircraft number (*Larry Tanberg Collection via Larry Hickey*)

This Type 1 Land-based Transport is just seconds away from being destroyed by the bomb seen falling in the foreground. Photographed at Babo, in western New Guinea, on 27 May 1944, the aircraft's tail code '052-03' has yet to be positively identified, although the G4M is believed to have belonged to the 25th *Tokubetsu Konkyochi-Tai* (Special Base Unit). This outfit was responsible for operating the bases in this part of western New Guinea (*Larry Tanberg Collection via Larry Hickey*)

redesignated 701 *Kokutai* (Second Formation) on 20 February, now had its flying echelon redesignated as K702. Later still, on 5 May, the flying echelon of 732 *Ku* became K707. Initially, these *hikotai* were all assigned back to the same parent *kokutai* which had spawned them, but some were later reassigned elsewhere.

The focus of air operations shifted now to New Guinea as American forces landed at Hollandia on 22 April. That same day 732 *Ku* deployed to Sorong, on the tip of western New Guinea, from Mindanao, where it was joined 24 hours later by a provisional unit made up of aircraft from both 761 and 755 *Ku*. The intensity of US air strikes on Sorong made operations from the base extremely difficult, and 761 and 755 *Ku* detachments had returned to their parent units in the Marianas by 1 May.

The American landings on Biak on 27 May provoked a major reaction from the Japanese, who mobilised Operation *Kon* in an effort to repel the enemy that had come ashore. That evening, 20 Type 1s of 732 and 753

Model 11 '05-333' of Attack *Hikotai* 705 (K705), 753 *Kokutai* crash-landed at Jefman/Samate (Sorong) and was photographed there on 16 June 1944. 753 *Ku*, along with 732 *Ku*, was active over western New Guinea during May and early June 1944, flying some very effective, albeit small-scale, night attacks against Wakde (*Stewart Malqvist Collection via Larry Hickey*)

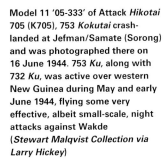

Ku advanced to Wasile, in the Halmaheras, from Digos (Davao Airfield No 3) on Mindanao, and on the night of the 28th, a force of 13 aircraft from the two units attacked shipping east of Biak with torpedoes. The results were uncertain, however, and five aeroplanes were lost. On the 31st, seven *rikko* again went after shipping off Biak with torpedoes, losing one of their number during the course of the mission.

Operating once more out of Sorong, night attacks in the area continued into early June, but attrition reduced them to small-scale raids, often by no more than two or three aircraft. But such raids could still do serious damage, especially against the American airfield on Wakde, half way between Hollandia and Biak, where US Fifth Air Force aeroplanes were crowded without adequate dispersal.

On the night of 5 June two Type 1s of 753 *Ku*, led by Ens Isao Sunayama, succeeded in destroying six aircraft and damaging 80 others on Wakde, whilst a second raid by three machines from the same unit on the night of the 8th did further damage.

On 11-12 June the focus returned to the Central Pacific once again when the Marianas came under heavy attack from US carrier task forces. The following day Saipan was shelled by American warships. The enemy was clearly about to launch a major invasion of the Mariana Islands, at the heart of the Japanese defence system in the Central Pacific. Biak and western New Guinea were now abandoned to the enemy as Combined Fleet began preparations for Operation *A-Go*, the long-awaited showdown with the US Pacific Fleet.

OPERATION *A-GO*

Elaborate preparations had been made for this decisive battle with the Americans, both by the carrier forces of Vice Adm Jisaburo Ozawa, and the land-based units of 1st Air Fleet. But by this time, enemy superiority proved overwhelming.

Early Model 22 (G4M2) '01-322' of Attack *Hikotai* 701 (K701), 755 *Kokutai* tries to escape the attention of US Navy fighters by diving towards the sea in the Central Pacific in May/June 1944. The new Model 22s had finally begun to reach combat units during early 1944, but by this time American superiority both in men and machines was so overwhelming that the *rikko* had little impact in its traditional attack role (*National Archives via James F Lansdale*)

The wreckage of a Model 24 (G4M2A) of Attack *Hikotai* 702 (K702) in the Philippines, probably at Clark Field, in late 1944. The aircraft is probably a Model 24 *Ko*, since it has waist gun positions for 20 mm cannon, although it does not appear to have carried radar. By this time, the traditional '300s' individual aircraft number range was no longer used in many *rikko* units. K702 fought longest in the Philippines during the 1944/45 campaign, arriving in late October 1944 and finally withdrawing to Taiwan in early January 1945. The markings reflect the *hikotai* number itself, the unit being assigned to 752 *Kokutai* until transferred to 763 *Ku* in mid-November (*David Pluth*)

This abandoned Model 24 of 762 *Kokutai* was almost certainly photographed at Clark Field in November 1944. It probably belonged to K703, which had transferred to 762 *Ku* on 10 October 1944 from 752 *Ku*. After seeing action against the US carrier task force off Taiwan in mid-October 1944, 762 *Ku* (with its two component *hikotai*, K708 and K703) deployed to the Philippines in mid-November 1944, but it stayed there for only a brief period (*Donald P Baker Collection via Larry Hickey*)

The main battle, fought between opposing carrier forces on 19-20 June 1944 ended in utter defeat for the Japanese, while their land-based air units were able to provide little support, being decimated at their bases by marauding US carrier aeroplanes before the main action was joined.

The feeling was now widespread that the Type 1 *Rikko* was long past its prime. With newer aircraft, such as the *Ginga* (Milky Way) Land-based Bomber (P1Y1 'Frances') coming on line, the Type 1 was relegated entirely to night missions and patrol duties. Type 1s of 761, 751, 755 and 753 *Kokutai* took part in the battle in small numbers from bases on Tinian, Guam and Peleliu. These units were later joined by a detachment of *rikko* from the Yokosuka *Kokutai* and 752 *Ku*, incorporated into a formation known as the Hachiman Unit (named after the Shinto War God), which was based at Iwo Jima. Despite the determination of their crews, the enemy's defences were now so formidable that the *rikko* had negligible impact.

Model 24 *Otsu* '763-12' of K702 (now reflecting assignment to 763 *Kokutai*) was captured intact by American forces at Clark Field in 1945. Note the overall dark green camouflage for night operations (*National Archives via Robert C Mikesh*)

Following annihilating losses in the Battle of the Philippine Sea, the IJN undertook a sweeping reorganisation of air units on 10 July 1944. Among *rikko* units, 732, 751, 753 and 755 *Kokutai* and Attack *Hikotai* 701, 705, 706 and 707 were disbanded. Those Type 1-equipped combat units remaining were K702, assigned to 701 *Ku*, K703, assigned to 752 *Ku*, K704, now assigned to 761 *Ku*, and K708, newly-formed on this date from the *hikotai* of 762 *Kokutai*, a *rikko* unit formed at Kanoya back on 15 February 1944.

Following the debacle in the Marianas, many in the Imperial Navy began to feel, privately, that the war was lost. It was now clear to all that conventional air operations against the American juggernaut would merely cause prohibitive losses for little result. Consensus now began to grow that altogether desperate measures were called for.

TAIWAN AND THE PHILIPPINES

Following defeat in the Marianas, K704 undertook operations from bases on Mindanao in September and early October 1944. K702, assigned to 752 *Kokutai* since September, arrived at Clark Field, on Luzon, in late October and joined K704 in the Philippines. However, with major attrition following the US landings at Leyte on 20 October, K704 returned to Japan the following month.

Meanwhile, K708 and K703 under 762 *Kokutai*, had been formed into a tactical formation known as *T-Butai*, or T-Force, in Japan. 'T' stood for 'typhoon', and the force's mission was to make attacks against the US carrier task forces using rough weather as a shield. The two *hikotai*, along with other units, expended themselves in a series of night attacks against the US fleet off Taiwan from between 12 and 14 October 1944.

A period of replenishment then ensued, during which time K703 carried out strikes against Marianas bases now being used by B-29s, flying its first mission there on 2 November. A fortnight later both K703 and K708 joined K702 at Clark Field, and at this time the latter unit left 752 *Ku* control and came under 763 *Kokutai*, which had been formed on 10 October 1944. The three *rikko hikotai* undertook a number of missions to Leyte, but by late November both K703 and K708 were back in Japan. Fighting on alone, K702 remained in the Philippines until the end of the air campaign, and then withdrew to Taiwan in January 1945.

This page
These close-up shots of '763-12' reveal details of Type 3 *Ku* Mark 6 (H6) radar side antennae, and 20 mm positions in the fuselage waist and tail. Prior to the installation of these short-barrelled Type 99 Mark 1 cannon in the fuselage waist, the gun positions were aligned with each other on both sides of the rear fuselage. However, once the larger 20 mm cannon were installed, the positions were offset, and the one on the port side was sited further forward than the one to starboard. With the *hinomaru* on both sides painted immediately aft of the 20 mm barrel stowage trough, these markings were similarly offset from each other. Some units painted the port side *hinomaru* off-centre from the circular rear fuselage hatch in order to align it with the *hinomaru* on the starboard side. Note the chalked 'BOOBY TRAPPED!' warning just to the left of the tail glazing in the photograph to right (*via Bunrindo K K and National Archives via Dana Bell*)

Upon its return to Japan from the Philippines, K704 took over from K703 and K708 on missions to the Marianas, sending out raids on 28 November and 7 December.

Following US landings on Iwo Jima on 19 February 1945, K704 flew out of Kisarazu and made night attacks. On 5 March it was assigned to 706 *Kokutai*, which was the last land attack *kokutai* to be formed. A final mission to Iwo Jima was flown on the night of 25/26 March, but thereafter, all air efforts were directed against Okinawa.

JINRAI – DIVINE THUNDER

In August 1944, Japan's desperate circumstances finally persuaded the Imperial Navy to develop a suicide weapon of the air. A rocket-powered glide bomb packing a 1200-kg warhead would have a devastating effect on any ship it struck, but the speedy development of a viable guidance system crucial to the success of such a weapon was beyond Japanese technology at the time. What they lacked in technology, however, the IJN decided to make up for in martial spirit. A human pilot would guide the weapon to its point of impact after being launched from a *rikko* mothership.

The design was finalised with unprecedented speed, and a production model was completed by September. Given the name *Ohka* (Cherry Blossom), volunteers were now sought to fly this macabre machine. Thus, even before the birth of the Kamikaze Special Attack Corps in the Philippines, there were airmen being trained to carry out deliberate one-way missions.

The last moments of a Model 24 *Tei* (G4M2E) of 2nd *Chutai*, K711, 721 *Kokutai*, caught on film by the gun camera of a US Navy F6F whilst still carrying its *Ohka* suicide rocket bomb. This aircraft was one of 18 *rikko* downed by Hellcats during the first *Jinrai* (Divine Thunder) sortie, flown on 21 March 1945
(*US Navy via Robert C Mikesh*)

On 1 October 1944, 721 *Kokutai* was formed as the first operational *Ohka* unit. 721's commander was Capt Motoharu Okamura, a veteran fighter pilot and ardent proponent of aerial *taiatari* (ramming) tactics. Lt Cdr Goro Nonaka, 752's leader of countless night torpedo attacks in the Central Pacific, came in as *hikotaicho*, and on 15 November the *Hiko-tai* became K711 under Nonaka's command. On 20 December Lt Cdr Jiro Adachi's K708 was transferred in from 762 *Ku* as a second land attack *hikotai* for 721 *Ku*. In keeping with their special nature, the *Ohka* operations were given the dramatic name of *Jinrai* (Divine Thunder).

Air Technical Arsenal Chief, Vice Adm Misao Wada, had made it clear that unless the *Rikko/Ohka* combination was used under conditions of local air superiority, there would be little hope for its success. The *Ohka* Model 11 weighed 2140 kg fully loaded, and carrying such a payload made the *Ohka's* specially-modified mothership – the Type 1 *Rikko* Model 24 *Tei* – extremely sluggish. The combination struggled to reach an altitude of 5000 metres at most, all the while consuming fuel at an alarming rate. There was every danger that the combination would be shot down long before the target came within effective *Ohka* range, which was a mere 20 nautical miles.

Having advanced to bases on Kyushu in February 1945, 721 *Ku* waited for a chance to strike. Great hopes were placed on the *Ohka*, but its operations were plagued by disaster from the start. On 18 March Usa-based K708 prepared to undertake the very first *Jinrai* operation. However, before the *Ohka*-laden *rikko* could take off, the base was attacked by US carrier aircraft. Nearly all the Type 1s were destroyed on the ground, and the mission was cancelled.

This Model 24 *Tei* of the 2nd *Chutai*, K711, 721 *Ku* is seen on the ground at Kanoya with an *Ohka* attached sometime prior to the ill-fated 21 March mission. With the aircraft carrying a 13 mm gun in the nose, the bomber's radar antenna has had to be repositioned from the nose tip to above the nose cone glazing (*via Bunrindo K K*)

On 21 March K711(led by Lt Cdr Nonaka) succeeded in launching 18 aircraft on the first *Jinrai* sortie, with 15 of the *rikko* carrying *Ohka* to give the weapon its combat debut. The IJN was under the impression that repeated attacks on the US carriers off Kyushu by other aircraft in the preceding three days had greatly weakened Task Force 58, but they were sadly mistaken.

Although 30 *Rei-sen* were sortied as escorts for the bombers, these were unable to fend off the American interceptors. Within 20 minutes all 18 Type 1s had been shot down by F6Fs of VF-17 and VBF-17 from USS *Hornet*, and not a single *Ohka* had been launched. Devastated by these losses, K711 was disbanded on 5 May, leaving K708 to take over as the operational *hikotai*. The latter unit would subsequently undertake a number of smaller scale *Jinrai* sorties, primarily at night, prior to the war's end.

OKINAWA

The Americans came ashore on Okinawa, on the very doorstep of Japan's Home Islands, on 1 April 1945. That night, K708 flew its first *Jinrai* mission with six *Ohka*-carrying *rikko*, and one mothership made it back to base. Two simply disappeared, another crashed and a fourth ditched, while the fifth set down on Taiwan and was lost during its return flight.

The Okinawa campaign triggered a blizzard of Japanese suicide sorties by aircraft of every description in a series of Special Attack operations known as *Kikusui* (Floating Chrysanthemum). However, aside from the *Jinrai* operations of 721 *Ku*, *rikko* sorties were limited to conventional attack missions in small numbers at night from bases on Kyushu and Taiwan.

Also flying from Kyushu was K704, which was controlled by 706 *Ku*, while 801 *Kokutai* (originally a flying boat unit) operated Reconnaissance (*Teisatsu*) *Hikotai* 703 (T703). Formerly K703, the latter unit had been redesignated on 15 March 1945. T707 and T709 were also assigned to 801 *Ku*, and they performed mainly night patrols and mine laying

Photographed at Konoike in 1945, Model 24 *Tei* '722-13' of 722 *Kokutai* is carrying an *Ohka* K-1 Training Glider, as evidenced by the landing skid which is just visible below the *Ohka*. 722 *Ku* was formed on 15 February 1945 as the second *Jinrai* unit, and it was intended to operate the jet-powered *Ohka* Model 22 in conjunction with the higher performance *Ginga* (P1Y1 'Frances') Land-based Bomber, which would act as a mothership. The war ended before the unit became operational, however (*via* S Nohara)

The wrecked remains of a Model 22 of the Omura Detachment of 951 *Kokutai* can be seen in front of the hangar at Omura following the end of the war. A few Type 1s were used for antisubmarine patrol work in units such as 951 *Ku*. Note the unusual triangular presentation of the unit code on the tail. In the left foreground are the remains of a Type 1 *Rikko*, tail marked '21-901', formerly of the transport unit 1021 *Kokutai* (*Author's Collection*)

operations. From Taiwan, K702, under 765 *Ku* control, flew a small number of missions, as did a provisional unit known as Attack (Special) *Hikotai* 701. Again part of 765 *Ku*, 701 was equipped with Type 1 aircraft, and personnel, that had been despatched to Taiwan from the Malaya and East Indies-based training unit 13th *Kokutai*.

K708 flew its next *Jinrai* sortie on the afternoon of 12 April with eight *rikko*, which succeeded in launching six *Ohka*. One of them sank the destroyer USS *Mannert L Abele* in the only confirmed sinking of an enemy vessel by *Ohka*. Five *rikko* motherships were lost, and a sixth crash-landed. A daylight mission on the 14th resulted in all seven *rikko* motherships being lost, while another daylight mission two days later by six aircraft resulted in four losses. K708 went back to flying at night after that, although small-scale missions continued into May.

On the night of 21 June, the tenth and last *Ohka* mission was flown by six *rikko*, four motherships failing to return. When daylight came on 22 June, all organised resistance by Lt Gen Ushijima's 32nd Army finally came to an end on Okinawa. However, conventional *rikko* attacks and patrols over Okinawa continued at a reduced pace until the end of the war. Indeed, the last Type 1 combat mission was flown by two machines of 801 *Kokutai* on the night of 12 August 1945, the aircraft attacking shipping off Okinawa.

OPERATION *TSURUGI*

By June 1945 Japan's major cities had been reduced to ashes by legions of B-29s flying from bases in the Marianas. These raids had to be stopped, if only temporarily, in an effort to complete preparations to meet the expected invasion of the Home Islands. Japanese army commandos had attempted just that when they attacked enemy airbases on Okinawa on

24 May 1945. The troops had been flown in at night aboard ten modified Type 97 Heavy Bombers (Ki-21 'Sally'), and the results had been encouraging enough for the IJN to plan a similar raid, but on a much larger scale. The navy was going to go after the B-29s at their bases in the Marianas.

On 24 June orders were formally issued for two interrelated actions, codenamed Operations *Tsurugi* (Sword) and *Retsu* (Ferocity). *Retsu* was to be a low-level attack on the B-29 bases by some 30 *Ginga* (P1Y1) bombers, half of them specially modified to carry up to 17 20 mm cannon – two forward-firing in the nose, and 15 obliquely-mounted and downward firing in the bomb-bay.

Retsu was to be followed by *Tsurugi*, in which 20 Type 1 *Rikko*, acting as transports, were to crash-land on the airfields and disgorge navy commandos. The latter would then set about destroying as many B-29s as possible on the ground, before fighting to the death. Many of the *rikko* were modified by having their dorsal turrets removed and the opening faired over. The aerial portion of the two operations was in the hands of 706 *Kokutai*, the *Ginga* under K405 and the Type 1s operated by K704. Training by the *rikko* for *Tsurugi* was concentrated at Misawa, and other bases in northern Honshu.

Preparations were elaborate. The commandos trained against full-scale wooden mock ups of B-29s, and captured Superfortress crews were interrogated for any useful information they might provide concerning

These Type 1 *Rikko* were photographed at Yokosuka soon after VJ-Day. Behind *'Yo-* 308' of the Yokosuka *Kokutai* is a Model 22 marked '3–*Ha'*, which formerly belonged to K704, 706 *Kokutai*, and was slated to take part in the still-born Operation *Tsurugi*. The latter mission would have seen commando troops flown to the B-29 bases on Saipan, Tinian and Guam in specially-modified Type 1 *Rikko*, where they would have set about destroying as many B-29s as possible. Note that this aircraft has had its dorsal turret removed and the opening faired over in preparation for this special mission. The *hinomaru* has also been painted out (*via Robert C Mikesh*)

Two Type 1 *Rikko* Model 24 *Otsu* provide the backdrop for an A6M5 Model 52 *Rei-sen* found in the main hangar at Misawa by US troops on 20 October 1945. These aircraft had also been modified as transports for *Tsurugi*, with the *rikko* on the left having had a small glass radome added in place of its turret (*National Archives via R C Mikesh*)

Overleaf
This Type 1 Land-based Transport (G6M1-L), flown by Lt Den Sudo, was the lead aircraft of the two-aeroplane flight that carried Lt Gen Kawabe's surrender delegation to Ie Shima on 19 August 1945. An electrical malfunction en route rendered the *rikko's* landing flaps inoperable, and Sudo had to use most of the 1000 m runway in order to come to a stop. These photographs give an excellent illustration of the small technical differences between the G6M1-L and the standard G4M1. Often overlooked is the considerably larger dorsal blister on the G6M1, initially designed to carry a 20 mm cannon for the 'wingtip escort' gunship role. The position and framing details of the waist sponsons also differ from those of the standard G4M1 *rikko* (*Both National Archives via R C Mikesh*)

the bases. All mission participants were issued special replica uniforms to disguise them as USAAF ground crew.

The operation was set to take place in late July, but carrier raids on northern Honshu bases, including Misawa, on 14-15 July resulted in major losses of aircraft, and the operation was postponed until the following month. Meanwhile, its scale was increased, as additional Type 1 *Rikko* were scraped together for a renewed effort, and army commandos added to the operation.

New plans also included the hijacking of a flyable B-29 to Japan by some of the *rikko* flight crew. A Superfortress crash site near Nagoya had yielded a complete B-29 flight manual, and the Japanese were supremely confident that they could operate the complex heavy bomber once it was aloft.

As it finally stood, 60 Type 1 *Rikko* prepared to transport 300 navy commandos of the 101st Kure Special Naval Landing Force, and 300 army commandos of the 1st Raiding Regiment, to the Marianas. The navy commandos were to hit Guam with 20 *rikko*, while the army men were to assault Saipan, also with 20 aircraft. Commandos of both services were to strike Tinian with ten *rikko* each, and any survivors of the operation were to regroup in the hills and commence guerrilla action against the bases.

Taking weather and moon phases into consideration, the operation was scheduled to take place between 19 and 23 August. But contemplating upwards of a million casualties in an invasion of Japan, the Americans had also decided that conventional methods alone were not enough to end the war.

On 6 August 1945, history's first atomic bomb was dropped on Hiroshima. Seventy-two hours later, a second bomb fell on Nagasaki.

That same day another large-scale carrier raid was flown against the northern Honshu airfields after Allied intelligence had got wind of Operation *Tsurugi*. Twenty-nine *Rikko* and twenty *Ginga* were destroyed. On 15 August Japan surrendered, and Operation *Tsurugi* (then only days away from launch) never took place.

FINAL FLIGHTS

On 19 August, veteran *rikko* pilot Lt Den Sudo of Yokosuka *Kokutai* led two aircraft off from Kisarazu. The lead aircraft, which Sudo flew, was a *rikko* transport version (G6M1-L), while the other was an old familiar Type 1 *Rikko* Model 11 (G4M1). At the direction of Gen Douglas MacArthur's headquarters, both had been painted white overall. Instructions had also called for prominent green crosses to be placed where the *hinomaru* had been painted out, and on the vertical tails. The crosses were very dark in colour, appearing black to the eye.

The aeroplanes carried a delegation of 16 passengers, headed by Lt Gen Torashiro Kawabe, as far as Ie Shima, the tiny island base off Okinawa. From there, Gen Kawabe and his delegation continued on to Manila in a USAAF C-54, where they received detailed instructions from the Allied command concerning the surrender.

The aircrew waited overnight on Ie Shima, and following the return of the delegates from Manila the next day, Sudo took off in the transport with the general and ten others. An unexpected fuel shortage during the return flight forced his aircraft down near the mouth of the Tenryu River, but no one was hurt. The second *rikko* had to stay on Ie Shima one more day for minor repairs, but it was then flown directly to Kisarazu on the 21st with the rest of Kawabe's party. So ended the last official mission of the Type 1 Land-based Attack Aircraft.

The last official mission, however, was not the final flight for the Type 1 *Rikko*. Having now received detailed surrender instructions from the Allies, the Imperial Navy command wished to disband the *Ohka*-slinging 'Divine Thunderers' of 721 *Kokutai* at the earliest opportunity. Given the special nature of the unit's operations, and the strong passions held by many in the unit, the navy was particularly anxious to avoid another rebellion as had occurred at Atsugi.

On 23 August, the last great gathering of airworthy Type 1 *Rikko* took place at Komatsu, in Ishikawa Prefecture, the final wartime base of 721 *Ku*. Once again, the base reverberated with the sound of *Kasei* engines as the *rikko* taxied out for take off. They would disperse to airfields throughout Japan, carrying surviving sons home to their families.

Hikocho Jiro Adachi stood by the command post in the late August heat and watched as they took off, one by one.

'As the last of them receded into the distance, then disappeared from view, I continued to stare after it, for a long, long time.'

Previous page
The second aircraft of the two-aeroplane surrender delegation was a standard Type 1 *Rikko* Model 11 (G4M1). The extra row of side windows along the nose, as well as additional small windows at the extreme rear fuselage, distinguish standard mid-production G4M1s from the G6M1, as well as early-production G4M1s. Both aircraft carried green crosses, those on the G4M1 being somewhat thicker, with shorter arms than those on the G6M1-L. The colour used for the crosses was a very dark green camouflage paint, which appeared black to the eye (*Both National Archives via R C Mikesh*)

APPENDICES

TYPE 1 LAND-BASED ATTACK AIRCRAFT UNITS OF THE IMPERIAL JAPANESE NAVY, 1941-45

Yokosuka *Kokutai*

Established 1/4/16. Oldest air unit in IJN. Came to operate all types of aircraft as special combat evaluation unit of IJN. Also fielded combat detachments overseas during 1944. Did not operate *rikko* after circa 7/44.

Kisarazu *Kokutai*

Established 1/4/36. fought in China. Training unit from 15/1/40. Began to receive Type 1 *Rikko* from 7/41. Returned to combat duty 1/4/42. Fought in New Guinea and Solomons. Redesignated 707 *Kokutai* 1/11/42, and continued combat based at Rabaul, but decimated in Guadalcanal campaign. Disbanded 1/12/42.

Kanoya *Kokutai* (first formation)

Established 1/4/36. Re-equipped with Type 1 *Rikko* 9/41. Took part in conquest of South-east Asia and sinking of HMS *Prince of Wales* and *Repulse*. Combat in New Guinea and Solomons from 9/42. Redesignated 751 *Ku* 1/10/42, and continued combat in Southeastern Area, later Central Pacific. K704 assigned as flying echelon 4/3/44. Disbanded 10/7/44.

Takao *Kokutai* (first formation)

Established 1/4/38. First unit to receive Type 1 *Rikko* 5/41. Took part in conquest of South-east Asia. Remained in East Indies following end of 1st Phase Operations. Flew missions over north-western Australia in 1942. Sent detachment to Rabaul in 9/42. Redesignated 753 *Kokutai* on 1/10/44, and remained in East Indies. Flew missions over Australia in 1943. Transferred to Central Pacific 12/43 to 1/44. Flying echelon became K705 1/4/44. Disbanded 10/7/44.

Chitose *Kokutai*

Established 1/10/39. Received first Type 1 *Rikko* 11/41, but remained equipped with Type 96 *Rikko*. Based in central Pacific. Gradually converted during course of first half 1942. Sent detachment to Rabaul in 9/42, entire unit then deployed there 10/42. Redesignated 703 *Kokutai* 1/11/42, and continued to fight at Rabaul, but suffered heavy attrition. Returned to Japan 12/42. Disbanded 15/3/43.

Misawa *Kokutai*

Established 10/2/42. Deployed to Rabaul 8/42. Redesignated 705 *Kokutai* 1/11/42, and continued to operate in Southeastern Area. Transferred to East Indies 11/43. Bombed Calcutta 5/12/43. Transferred to Peleliu 2/44. Flying echelon made independent as K706 4/3/44. 705 *Ku* ceased to be *rikko* unit at this time.

Shinchiku *Kokutai*

Established 1/4/42 as *rikko* training unit, taking over function of Kisarazu *Kokutai*, returned to combat duty on same date. Heavy enemy raid on Shinchiku caused training there to be curtailed. Training transferred to Kanoya *Kokutai* (second formation). Disbanded 1/1/44.

Kanoya *Kokutai* (second formation)

Established 1/10/42 as an operational training unit for carrier bomber and carrier attack aeroplane personnel. *Rikko* training function added 1/1/44, but transferred to Toyohashi *Kokutai* on 10/7/44, Kanoya *Ku* (second formation) disbanded same day.

Takao *Kokutai* (second formation)

Trained *rikko* observers from 1/1/44 to 15/6/44.

Toyohashi *Kokutai* (first formation)

Established 1/4/43 as *rikko* crew training unit. Redesignated 701 *Kokutai* (second formation) 20/2/44 and operated in northern Japan from 3/44. Flying echelon became K702 1/4/44. With reassignment of K702 on 18/9/44, it ceased to be a *rikko* unit.

Toyohashi *Kokutai* (second formation)

Established 10/7/44 as *rikko* crew training unit with personnel from Kanoya *Kokutai* (second formation). Ceased training function 5/45. Deployed combat detachment for Okinawa campaign in 1945.

Miyazaki *Kokutai*

Established 1/12/43 as *rikko* operational training unit. Flying echelon transferred to Matsushima *Kokutai*. Disbanded 1/8/44.

Matsushima *Kokutai*

Established 1/8/44 with personnel from Miyazaki *Kokutai*. Conducted *rikko* crew training until end of war. Deployed combat detachment during Okinawa campaign in 1945.

No 2 Takao *Kokutai* (not to be confused with Takao *Kokutai* second formation)

Established 15/8/44 as air gunner specialist training unit. Disbanded 15/2/45.

San'a *Kokutai*

Established 1/10/43 as *rikko* pilot training unit. Transferred this function to Oryu *Kokutai* in early 1944.

Oryu *Kokutai*

Early 1944 took over *rikko* training function of San'a *Kokutai*. Disbanded 1/5/44.

4th *Kokutai*

Established 10/2/42. Fought in Southeastern Area until withdrawn to Japan 9/42. Redesignated 702 *Kokutai* 1/11/42 and redeployed to Rabaul 5/43. Disbanded 1/12/43.

13th *Kokutai* (second formation)

Took over training functions from Oryu *Kokutai* 1/5/44. Took part in limited combat operations. Absorbed by 381 *Kokutai* 15/1/45.

752 *Kokutai*

Redesignation of 1st *Kokutai* on 1/11/42. Re-equipped with Type 1 *Rikko* during spring 1943. Operated in Northern Theatre 5/43. Sent detachment to Rabaul 7-9/43. Redeployed to Central Pacific 11/43. Reformed in Japan 2/44. Flying echelon became K703 on 1/4/44. Thereafter operated various *hikotai* and remained on active status until end of war.

755 *Kokutai*

Redesignation of Genzan *Kokutai* on 1/11/42. Last *rikko* unit to re-equip with Type 1, doing so 9-10/43. Active in Central Pacific during Gilberts and Marshalls campaigns 11/43 to 2/44. Flying echelon reorganised 4/3/44. Assigned K701 and K706. Disbanded 10/7/44 following Marianas campaign.

761 *Kokutai*

Established 1/7/44. Known initially as *Ryu Butai* (Dragon Unit). First unit to receive G4M2. Fought in Central Pacific and western New Guinea. Ended war as a ground unit in the Philippines.

732 *Kokutai*

Established 1/10/43. Operated as Operational training unit in Malaya from 12/43. Became combat unit and fought in western New Guinea from 4/44. Flying echelon became K707 on 5/5/44. Disbanded 10/7/44.

762 *Kokutai*

Established 15/2/44. Flying echelon became K708 on 10/7/44. Took part in air operations off Taiwan in 10/44 and the Philippines in 11/44. Operated thereafter from bases in Kyushu until end of war.

763 *Kokutai*

Established 10/10/44 as a *Ginga* (P1Y1) unit. Added Type 1 *Rikko*-equipped K702 in 11/44. Ended war as ground unit in Philippines.

765 *Kokutai*

Established 5/2/45 at Tainan and remained on

Taiwan until end of war. Operated a variety of aircraft, including K702's following latter *kokutai's* withdrawal from the Philippines.

721 *Kokutai*
Established 1/10/44 as first *Jinrai* unit, operating *Ohka* rocket bombs. Flying echelon became K711 on 15/11/44. K708 added 20/12/44. Last *Ohka* mission flown 21/6/45.

722 *Kokutai*
Established 15/2/45 as second *Jinrai* unit, scheduled to operate jet-powered *Ohka* Model 22, but failed to reach operational status before end of war.

706 *Kokutai*
Established 5/3/45. Last *kokutai* to operate *rikko* to be formed during war, with K704

assigned. Planned to launch Operation *Tsurugi* against B-29 bases, but war ended before mission was undertaken.

801 *Kokutai*
Originally a flying boat unit. Operated *rikko* from 1/1/45 following the assignment of K703. Added T707 on 15/3/45. Served exclusively as a *rikko* patrol unit from 4/45 until the end of the war.

1001 *Kokutai*
Established 1/7/43 as first specialised transport *kokutai* in IJN. Active in transport and ferry role until end of war.

1021 *Kokutai*
Established as transport unit 1/1/44. Absorbed by 1081 *Kokutai* 15/7/45.

1081 *Kokutai*
Established as transport unit 1/4/44.

1022 *Kokutai*
Established as transport unit 10/7/44.

1023 *Kokutai*
Established as transport unit 1/10/44. Unit was disbanded 5/3/45.

901 *Kokutai*
Maritime escort unit established 15/12/43.

903 *Kokutai*
Maritime escort unit established 15/12/44.

951 *Kokutai*
Maritime escort unit established 15/12/44.

TOKUSETSU (SPECIAL ESTABLISHMENT) *HIKOTAI*

Attack *Hikotai* 701 (K701)
Formed 4/3/44 from flying echelon of 755 and 751 *Kokutai*. Assigned to 755 *Ku*. Fought in Central Pacific. Disbanded 10/7/44.

Attack *Hikotai* (Special) 701
A provisional *hikotai* formed from elements of 13th *Kokutai*. Deployed to Taiwan and assigned to 765 *Kokutai*. Took part in Okinawa campaign from 4/45.

Attack *Hikotai* 702 (K702)
Formed 1/4/44 from flying echelon of 701 *Kokutai* (second formation). Reassigned to 752 *Ku* 9/44. Advanced to the Philippines 10/44. Reassigned to 763 *Ku* 11/44. Withdrew to Taiwan 1/45. Reassigned to 765 *Ku* 2/45.

Attack *Hikotai* 703 (K703)
Formed 1/4/44 from flying echelon of 752 *Kokutai*. Took part in Marianas campaign as part of *Hachiman* Unit. Reassigned to 762 *Kokutai* 10/10/44. Fought in air battle off Taiwan and in the Philippines. Returned to Japan and reassigned to 801 *Kokutai* 12/44. Redesignated Reconnaissance *Hikotai* 703 (T703) 15/3/45. Took part in Okinawa campaign.

Attack *Hikotai* 704 (K704)
Formed 4/3/44 from flying echelon of 755 and 751 *Kokutai*, and assigned to 751 *Ku*. Fought at Peleliu. Reassigned to 761 *Kokutai* 10/7/44. Fought over western New Guinea and the Philippines. Reassigned to 752 *Ku* 15/11/44, reformed in Japan. Reassigned to 706 *Kokutai* 12/3/45. Preparing for Operation *Tsurugi* when war ended.

Attack *Hikotai* 705 (K705)
Formed 1/4/44 from flying echelon of 753 *Kokutai*. Fought in western New Guinea. Disbanded 10/7/44.

Attack *Hikotai* 706 (K706)
Formed 4/3/44 from flying echelon of 705 *Kokutai*, and assigned to 755 *Kokutai*. Fought in Central Pacific. Disbanded 10/7/44.

Attack *Hikotai* 707 (K707)
Formed 5/5/44 from flying echelon of 732 *Kokutai*. Fought in western New Guinea and Central Pacific. Disbanded 10/7/44.

Attack *Hikotai* 708 (K708)
Formed 10/7/44 from flying echelon of 762

Kokutai. Fought in air battles off Taiwan and in the Philippines. Returned to Japan. Reassigned to 721 *Kokutai* 20/12/44. Flew *Jinrai* missions with *Ohka* during Okinawa campaign 4-6/45.

Attack *Hikotai* 711 (K711)
Formed from flying echelon of 721 *Kokutai* 15/11/44. Following disastrous first *Jinrai* sortie on 21/3/45, acted as training unit for K708 until disbanded 5/5/45.

Reconnaissance *Hikotai* 707 (T707)
Redesignation of T3 of 801 *Kokutai* on 15/3/45. Operated *rikko* on night patrol duties whilst assigned to 801 *Ku*.

Reconnaissance *Hikotai* 709 (T709)
Formed 5/3/45 as a night reconnaissance unit and assigned to 752 *Kokutai*. Operated under 801 *Kokutai* 4/45, but took heavy losses. Returned to 752 *Ku* and disbanded 5/5/45.

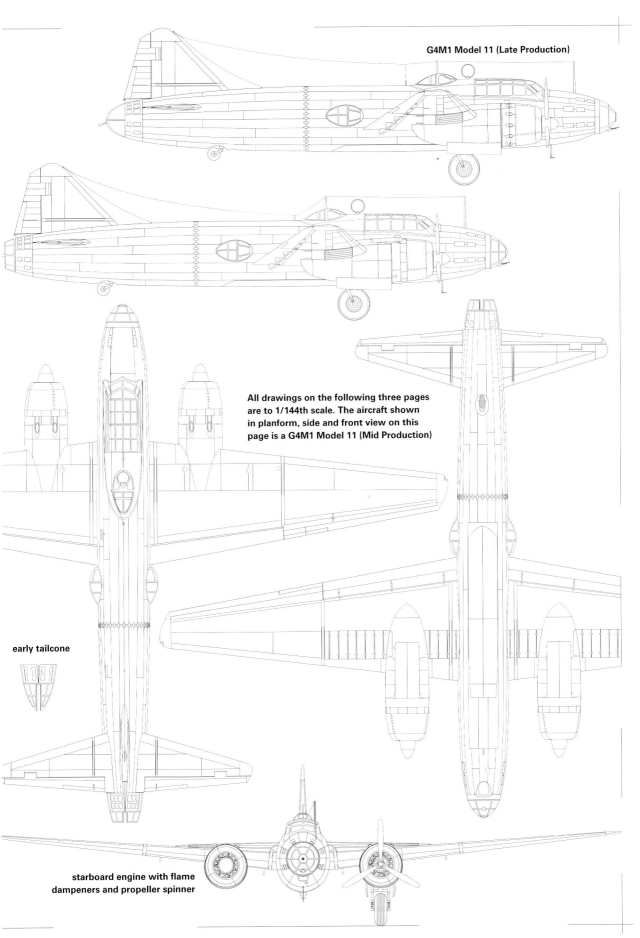

G4M1 Model 11 (Late Production)

All drawings on the following three pages are to 1/144th scale. The aircraft shown in planform, side and front view on this page is a G4M1 Model 11 (Mid Production)

early tailcone

starboard engine with flame dampeners and propeller spinner

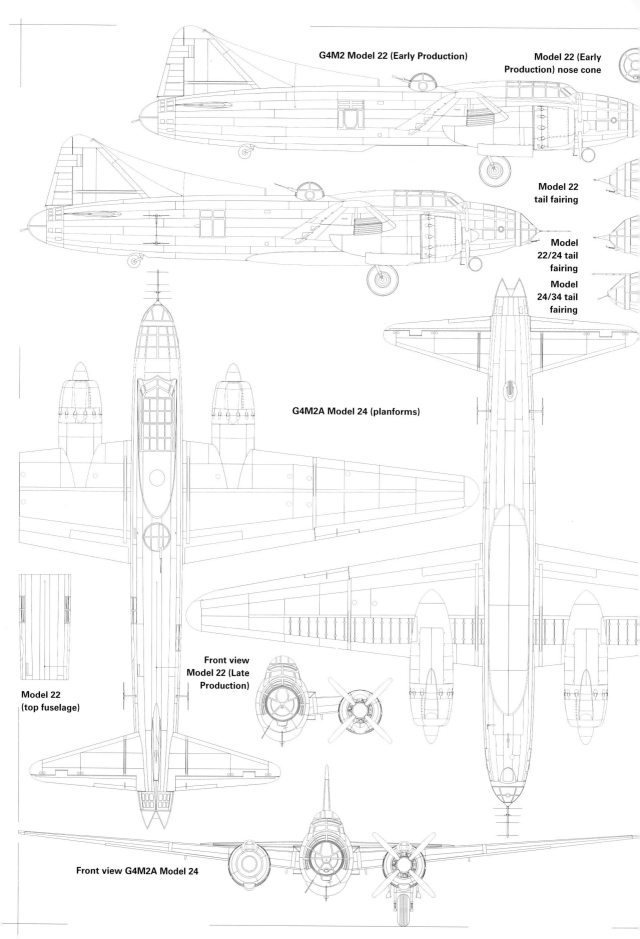

G4M2 Model 22 (Early Production)

Model 22 (Early Production) nose cone

Model 22 tail fairing

Model 22/24 tail fairing

Model 24/34 tail fairing

G4M2A Model 24 (planforms)

Model 22 (top fuselage)

Front view Model 22 (Late Production)

Front view G4M2A Model 24

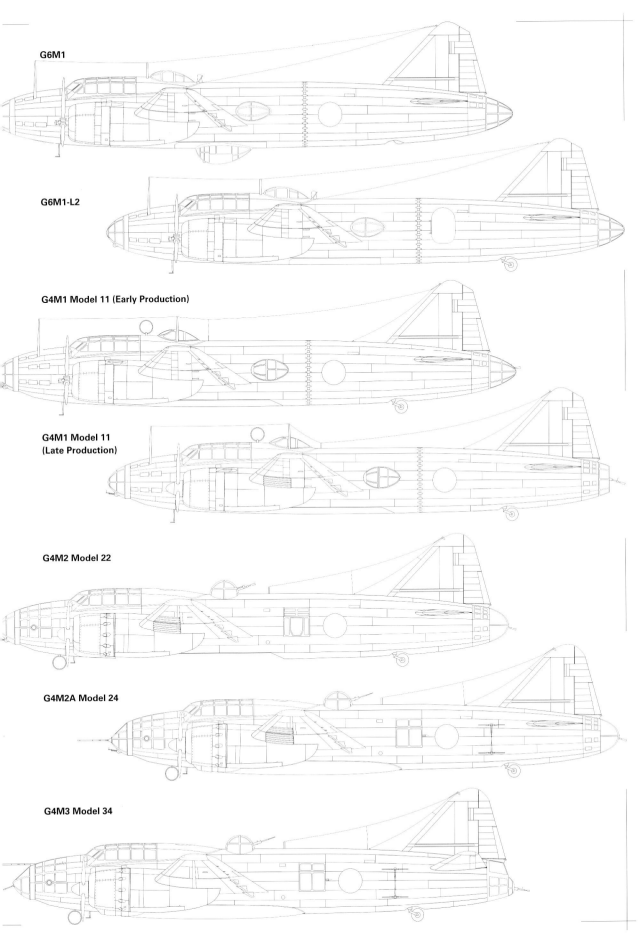

G6M1

G6M1-L2

G4M1 Model 11 (Early Production)

G4M1 Model 11
(Late Production)

G4M2 Model 22

G4M2A Model 24

G4M3 Model 34

COLOUR PLATES

1

G6M1 Ko-G6-6 (s/n 706) of Takao Kokutai, Yokosuka, Japan, and Takao, Taiwan, December 1940

The sixth G6M1 produced, this aircraft was one of three such machines ferried from the Air Technical Arsenal at Yokosuka, Japan, to Takao (Kao-hsiung), Taiwan, at the end of December 1940 for assignment to the Takao Kokutai as transition trainers for the G4M1. Originally built as 'wingtip escorts', these aircraft were never used in this role, being employed instead as transition trainers for the G4M1. It was not until April 1941 that both the G4M1 and the G6M1 were officially adopted for service use, with the latter being designated the Type 1 Land-based Large Trainer Model 11. Shown in the scheme it wore at the time of its ferry flight to Taiwan, the aircraft still carried Koku Gijutsu Sho (abbreviated to Kugisho) tail markings. These consisted of the katakana letter Ko for Koku Gijutsu Sho, followed by an abbreviated representation of the aircraft's technical short code designation and the sequential number of the aircraft as officially accepted by the navy. This machine remains in natural metal finish with red tail surfaces, which was the standard finish for most IJN aircraft up to the spring of 1941.

2

G4M1 K-384 of Kanoya Kokutai, Davao, the Philippines, January 1942

When the Pacific War was launched, all rikko wore a two-tone camouflage of dark green and medium brown on their upper surfaces, this scheme having been originally introduced for field operations in China. There were two basic patterns which were mirror images of each other, while the undersurfaces remained in natural metal finish. As this aircraft clearly shows, the Roman alphabet letter 'K' was used by Kanoya Kokutai as its unit code from November 1940 through to November 1942, while the individual aircraft number in the 300s signified its 'attack' role. At the start of the Pacific War, the Kanoya Kokutai had six chutai within its ranks. Individual aircraft numbers were allocated sequentially, and it is believed that the number blocks assigned were as follows – 1st Chutai 301 to 315, 2nd Chutai 316 to 330, 3rd Chutai 331 to 345, 4th Chutai 346 to 360, 5th Chutai 361 to 375 and 6th Chutai 376 to 390. Unlike the units operating single-engined aircraft, which used tail stripes to denote command status, rikko-equipped units employed these markings to show chutai affiliation. The number of stripes did not always correspond to the chutai number. In the Kanoya Kokutai during this period, the absence of stripes on the tail indicated 1st Chutai, whilst the 2nd Chutai carried a single horizontal stripe midway up the tail above the code. The 3rd Chutai is believed to have carried a double stripe, and the 4th Chutai employed a single stripe close to the

tail tip in order to distinguish it from the 2nd Chutai. 5th Chutai carried two stripes widely spaced apart to distinguish it from the 3rd, and the 6th Chutai used three stripes, two of which were close together in the same position as the 3rd Chutai and the third stripe spaced slightly apart near the top of the tail. 6th Chutai machine K-384 is shown as it appeared in January 1942, shortly after the unit had advanced to newly-captured Davao airfield, on the southern Philippine island of Mindanao. The single stripe on the rear fuselage denotes that the Kanoya Kokutai was originally assigned to the 1st Rengo Kokutai (Combined Kokutai), which later became the 21st Koku Sentai (Air Flotilla). This marking should not be confused with the 'combat stripe' used in the early stages of the China War by both services, and then exclusively by the JAAF during the Pacific War.

3

G4M1 T-361 of Takao Kokutai, Kupang, Timor, March 1942

Code letter 'T' was used by Takao Kokutai from November 1940 through to November 1942. Although frontline rikko began the Pacific War in the two-tone China finish, by late 1941 new aircraft were leaving the assembly line in overall uppersurface green camouflage, this scheme being devised for the 'Southern Operations'. These aircraft began to reach operational units in early 1942, and T-361 (an aircraft of the Takao's 5th Chutai) is one of the earliest examples for which the underlying photographic evidence can be specifically dated. When the Pacific War began, Takao Kokutai, like Kanoya Kokutai, was a large organisation with six chutai. The assignment of individual number blocks to the chutai is believed to have been the same as in Kanoya Kokutai.

4

G4M1 T-315 of Takao Kokutai, Clark Field, the Philippines, March/April 1942

This aircraft is painted in the rarer two-tone upper surface pattern where the demarcation line between the colours ran in the opposite direction from the more common scheme. The light-coloured band along the leading edge of the vertical fin is a replacement panel which has not yet been painted over. The low individual aircraft number and lack of tail stripe indicate that this aircraft was assigned to the 1st Chutai, which was engaged in bombing remnant American and Filipino forces on Corregidor at this time. The aeroplane's finish is well worn, reflecting the preceding three months of heavy combat.

5

G4M1 F-348 of 4th Kokutai, Rabaul, New Britain, 20 February 1942

This aircraft was commanded by Lt Cdr Takuzo Ito during the disastrous attack on USS Lexington on

20 February 1942. Its demise has been immortalised in a famous photo sequence (see pages 36-37) taken from the carrier during its attempted suicide dive on the vessel. The *Rikko* had earlier been fatally damaged by Lt Edward H 'Butch' O'Hare, who had succeeded in shooting its port engine nacelle clean off with his F4F-3. An ex-Takao *Kokutai* machine, this aircraft still wears two-tone brown and green camouflage. The white horizontal tail stripes, often mistaken for command stripes, denote its *chutai* affiliation within the *kokutai*, whilst the 'F' in 'F-348' was the unit code letter assigned to 4th *Kokutai* from its formation in February 1942 until November of that year.

6
G4M1 F-378 of 4th *Kokutai*, Rabaul, New Britain, 7 May 1942
Commanded by FPO1/c Misao Sugii, this aircraft participated in the torpedo attack on Adm Crace's cruiser support force during the Battle of the Coral Sea, and ditched at DeBoyne Reef immediately after the action. Its high individual tail number possibly denotes its assignement to 4th *Chutai*, although the single tail stripe is believed to have been a 2nd *Chutai* marking. With the 4th *Ku* suffering heavy attrition throughout its combat career, number sequences quickly became confused within the *kokutai*.

7
G4M1 H-324 of Misawa *Kokutai*, Saipan, Mariana Islands, 10 July 1942
Code letter 'H' was assigned to Misawa *Kokutai* from its formation in February 1942 until November 1942. This aircraft, handed down from Kanoya *Kokutai*, still wears a rather worn two-tone scheme of green and brown. Misawa *Kokutai* used a unique system of *chutai* markings, with a white tail tip indicating 1st *Chutai*, a broad horizontal band 2nd *Chutai* and a broad vertical band 3rd *Chutai*. Number blocks assigned were 301 to 319 for 1st *Chutai*, 320 to 339 for 2nd *Chutai* and 350 to 369 for 3rd *Chutai*.

8
G4M1 H-305 of Misawa *Kokutai*, Saipan, Mariana Islands, 7 August 1942
Original equipment of the Misawa *Kokutai* consisted of a mixture of older aircraft in two-tone green and brown and newer machines painted in overall green upper surface camouflage. One of the newer aircraft operated by the *kokutai*, 'H-305' is from the 1st *Chutai*, as denoted by the low number sequence and white tail tip. These markings are representative of Misawa *Kokutai* on the eve of the Guadalcanal campaign.

9
G4M1 353 of Misawa *Kokutai*, Rabaul, New Britain, 28 September 1942
By the second month of the Guadalcanal campaign the unit code 'H' had been painted out for security reasons in this active combat theatre.

Note also that by this time, the fuselage *hinomaru* featured a thin white edge. As detailed in profile seven, the broad vertical band on the tail of this *rikko* indicated its allocation to 3rd *Chutai*. One of the newer Model 11s issued to the *kokutai*, the aircraft had additional windows on the lower half of the rear fuselage, just ahead of the tail gun position. These windows were only present along the upper half of the rear fuselage on earlier *rikko*.

10
G4M1 R-360 of Kisarazu *Kokutai*, Rabaul, New Britain, September 1942
The code letter 'R' was used by *rikko* of Kisarazu *Kokutai*, with the two horizontal tail stripes believed to denote the unit's 3rd *Chutai*. The single white rear fuselage stripe harked back to the unit's days under the control of 1st Rengo *Kokutai*. Kisarazu *Kokutai* deployed to Rabaul in August, 1942, but was decimated in the Guadalcanal campaign and disbanded on 1 December 1943 following redesignation as 707 *Kokutai*.

11
G4M1 W2-373 of 752 *Kokutai*, Kisarazu, Japan, April 1943
1st *Kokutai* was redesignated 752 *Kokutai* on 1 November 1942. A new unit code system was also adopted at this time, with 'W' denoting the parent 24th *Koku Sentai* and the following numeral '2' indicating and aircraft from the second unit within the *koku sentai*. The one thick and one thin stripe combination was employed by 4th *Chutai*, whilst 1st *Chutai* had one thin diagonal stripe, 2nd *Chutai* two thin diagonal stripes and 3rd *Chutai* three thin diagonal stripes. Note the aircraft's propeller spinners, which began to appear on Model 11s from the summer of 1942 onwards. The external rubber pads on the wing undersurfaces were fitted on the production line (from March 1943) in an effort to increase fuel tank protection, while the flame dampeners carried by this particular aircraft were also a recent addition.

12
G4M1 323 (s/n 2656) of 705 *Kokutai*, Rabaul, New Britain, 18 April 1943
Misawa *Kokutai* was redesignated 705 *Kokutai* on 1 November 1942, and one of its most historic Type 1 *Rikko* was this aircraft, flown by FCPO Takashi Kotani. Its fame came from the fact that it was the aircraft in which Adm Isoroku Yamamoto, Commander-in-Chief Combined Fleet, was shot down in over Bougainville, in the Solomon Islands. It is reported that the *rikko* carried no *chutai* markings. The white square presentation for the fuselage *hinomaru* was characteristic for the Type 1 during this period. Built in March 1943, this aircraft was one of the last to reach the frontline without underwing rubber pads.

13
G4M1 336 (s/n 5749) of 705 *Kokutai*, Rabaul, New Britain, June 1943

By this time the *chutai* stripes on 705 *Ku* aircraft had become thinner than the style used in the old Misawa *Kokutai* days. It is believed that the horizontal stripe continued to denote 2nd *Chutai*, although the unit now had a four-*chutai* structure. This aircraft crash-landed on New Georgia during the Central Solomons campaign, apparently following the disastrous torpedo attack on Allied shipping on 30 June 1943.

14

G4M1 Z2-310 of 751 *Kokutai*, Rabaul, New Britain, July 1943

Kanoya *Kokutai* was redesignated 751 *Kokutai* on 1 October 1942, and under the new code system introduced for combat units in the autumn of 1942, 'Z' indicated 21st *Koku Sentai*. This aircraft belonged to 1st *Chutai*, which was sent down to Rabaul as emergency reinforcement in July 1943 while the rest of 751 *Ku* undertook rest and reformation on Tinian, in the Mariana Islands.

15

G4M1 351 of 702 *Kokutai*, Rabaul, New Britain, 12 October 1943

4th *Kokutai* was redesignated 702 *Kokutai* on 1 November 1942 and given the unit code 'U2', although following its redeployment to Rabaul in May 1943, the unit code was deleted – a common security measure in the Southeastern Area. The single horizontal stripe across the rudder only signified 3rd *Chutai*, 1st *Chutai* using a single horizontal stripe that ran across the entire fin and rudder, along with tail numbers in the 301 to 319 range. 2nd *Chutai* aircraft had a double horizontal stripe across the fin and rudder, and numbers in the 320 to 339 range. Aside from the single horizontal stripe on the rudder only, 3rd *Chutai* used numbers ranging from 340 to 359. Finally, 4th *Chutai rikko* were adorned with one thick and one thin horizontal stripe on the rudder only, and numbers in the 360 to 379 range. This aircraft is a late production Model 11, with individual engine exhaust stacks and a redesigned tail gun position more commonly seen on later G4M2 Model 22s.

16

G4M1 367 of 702 *Kokutai*, Rabaul, New Britain, 24 October 1943

Another example of a late production Model 11 of 702 *Ku*, this time from 4th *Chutai*, as indicated by one thick and one thin horizontal stripe across the rudder only. This system of *chutai* stripes in which some units were distinguished by having stripes across the rudder only was unique to 702 *Ku*.

17

G4M1 321 of 702 *Kokutai*, Rabaul, New Britain, November 1943

This 2nd *Chutai* aircraft was flown by Lt(jg) Hidezumi Maruyama, with FCPO Shoji Sekine as observer/navigator. On the night of 12/13 November 1943, Maruyama led a torpedo attack against US warships operating off Cape Torokina,

on Bougainville, and scored a hit on the light cruiser USS *Denver*. The *rikko* made it back to base despite being seriously damaged by AA fire (380+ flak holes were counted). Upon its return, '321' was deemed to be irreparable.

18

G4M1 324 of 751 *Kokutai*, Rabaul, New Britain, October 1943

Flown by FCPO Jitsuyoshi Kuramasu, this aircraft was a replacement machine received on 20 October 1943. The pilot's previous aircraft (an older standard Model 11 also numbered 324) had been destroyed on the ground at West Field, Rabaul (Vunakanau), during the US Fifth Air Force raid of 12 October 1943. That machine had been the sole surviving Type 1 to return to base from a daylight torpedo attack on an Allied convoy off Finschhafen, New Guinea, on 22 September 1943.

19

G4M1 52-008 of 752 *Kokutai*, Chitose Air Base, Hokkaido, Japan, September 1943

In August 1943 the letter/number unit code system gave way to a simple system reflecting the last two digits of the unit designation itself as the tail code. Also, at about this time 752 *Ku* discarded the hitherto standard three-digit individual aircraft number system in which the hundreds digit reflected the aircraft mission role (300s in the case of attack aircraft). Instead, 752 *Ku* adopted a single or double digit sequential numbering system, but added a '0' to the number to maintain three digits. The single diagonal tail stripe and individual number '008' denote a machine of 1st *Chutai*.

20

G4M1 52-059 of 752 *Kokutai*, Eniwetok, Marshall Islands, November/December 1943

An example of an aircraft from 3rd *Chutai* in the new marking scheme adopted by 752 *Ku*, with three diagonal stripes indicating its *chutai* allocation. Individual number block assignments were 001 to 019 for 1st *Chutai*, 020 to 039 for 2nd *Chutai*, 040 to 059 for 3rd *Chutai* and 060 to 079 for 4th *Chutai*. 752 *Kokutai* saw considerable action in the Gilberts and Marshall Islands campaigns of late 1943/early 1944, and was noted for its night torpedo attacks on US warships.

21

G4M1 52-073 (55-353) of 752 *Kokutai*, Eniwetok, Marshall Islands, January/February 1944

This aircraft reflects previous ownership by 755 *Ku*, and was subsequently taken over by 752 *Ku* in the field – the one thick and one thin tail stripe denote 4th *Chutai*. 752 *Ku*'s *chutai* marking system remained constant throughout the unit's wartime career, and was always presented diagonally.

22

G4M2 *Ryu* 41 of 761 *Kokutai*, Peleliu, Palau Islands March 1944

761 *Kokutai* was the first unit to equip with the

G4M2 Model 22. As part of the 1st *Koku Kantai* (second formation), the unit was given a name as well as a number, being known as the *Ryu-Butai* or 'Dragon Unit'. Its aircraft sported the *kanji* character *ryu* (dragon) on the tail, with a two-digit individual aircraft number beneath. Once deployed overseas, many aircraft deleted the *kanji* character and simply retained the two-digit aircraft number.

23
G4M2 06-303 of 706/755 *Kokutai*, Truk, Caroline Islands, March/April 1944
On 4 March 1944 the IJN reorganised the *kokutai* structure and divided the air and ground echelon functions. Henceforth, air echelons (*hikotai*) were given independent numerical designations, and were freely transferred from one *kokutai* to another as the tactical situation demanded. Aircraft of these independent *hikotai* often carried tail designators reflecting the *hikotai* number rather than that of the parent *kokutai*. As the air echelon of 705 *Ku*, Attack *Hikotai* 706 (often abbreviated to K706) was given a newly independent existence and assigned to 755 *Kokutai*. However, it continued to use the same system of *chutai* identification as had been previously employed, hence the white tail tip on this aircraft.

24
G4M2 01-312 of 701/755 *Kokutai*, Guam, Mariana Islands, April 1944
Attack *Hikotai* 701 was formed from personnel of 755 and 751 *Ku* at Truk on 4 March 1944 and assigned back to 755 *Ku*. As with K706's '06-303', the markings worn by this aircraft reflected the designation of its *hikotai*. K701 took over patrol duties from the latter unit at Truk in mid-May 1944, but was disbanded on 10 July 1944 (along with K706) following losses in the Marianas campaign.

25
G4M2A 752-12 of Attack *Hikotai* 703/752 *Kokutai*, Kisarazu Air Base, Japan, September 1944
Attack *Hikotai* 703 was formed from the flying echelon of 752 *Kokutai* on 1 April 1944 and then assigned back to 752 *Ku*. This particular aircraft was issued to the unit following its withdrawal to Kisarazu to reform in the wake of action in the Marianas Campaign, where K703 had flown from Iwo Jima as part of the *Hachiman* Unit. Its markings reflect the *kokutai* rather than the *hikotai* designation, with all three digits of the unit number being shown. The aircraft carries Type 3 *Ku* Mark 6 (H6) search radar, and is finished in dark green overall, denoting the nocturnal nature of its operations. Note that the *hinomaru* on the port fuselage side is no longer aligned with the circular rear fuselage hatch as had been the case in the past, but is offset to the rear. This allowed it to remain aligned with the *hinomaru* on the opposite side when the waist gun positions on the standard Model 24 were offset to accommodate 20 mm cannon.

26
G4M2A 762K-84 of Attack *Hikotai* 708/762 *Kokutai*, Tsuiki Air Base, Kyushu, Japan, September/October 1944
Attack *Hikotai* 708 was formed from the flying echelon of 762 *Ku* on 10 July 1944 and then immediately assigned back to *kokutai*. The letter 'K' on the tail stood for *kogeki* (attack), which was a marking often used by *rikko hikotai* during this period. The aircraft is shown just prior to the major actions against the US carrier task force off Taiwan in mid-October 1944 as part of 'T' Force. Note again the *hinomaru* offset from the rear fuselage hatch in order to align it with the *hinomaru* on the other side.

27
G4M2A 763-12 (s/n 12134) of Attack *Hikotai* 702/763 *Kokutai*, Clark Field, the Philippines, November/December 1944
Attack *Hikotai* 702, previously assigned to 701 *Kokutai* (second formation) and 752 *Kokutai*, became the last remaining *rikko* unit in the Philippines, continuing to fight in-theatre until early January 1945. From November 1944 K702 came under 763 *Ku* control, and following its withdrawal to Taiwan, 765 *Ku* took over. This particular aircraft was captured intact by US forces at Clark Field and was later repaired and test flown. Unit markings reflected the *kokutai* level of organisation. The port side fuselage *hinomaru* was concentric with the rear fuselage hatch, indicating that it was not aligned with the *hinomaru* on the opposite side. This means that the starboard side *hinomaru* was, therefore, positioned closer to the tail than the one to port.

28
G4M2E/MXY 7 721-305 of Attack *Hikotai* 711/721 *Kokutai*, Kanoya Air Base, Kyushu, Japan, 21 March 1945
This aircraft was one of eighteen motherships involved in the first combat sortie of the *Ohka* suicide rocket bomb, and was shot down by US Navy F6Fs along with the rest of its squadron-mates. The single white tail flash indicated a machine of Attack *Hikotai* 711's 1st *Chutai* (or *Buntai*). The aircraft carried its radar antenna above the nose cone glazing rather than in the nose tip, which meant that it had a nose-mounted 13 mm gun fitted. This modification meant that the aircraft was a standard Model 24 *Hei* converted into Model 24 *Tei*.

29
G4M2E/MXY 7 721-328 of Attack *Hikotai* 711/721 *Kokutai*, Kanoya Air Base, Kyushu, Japan, 21 March 1945
The disastrous 21 March 1945 sortie was undertaken by aircraft of K711's 1st and 2nd *Chutai*. The aircraft is also believed to have taken part in the mission, its two white flashes on the tail indicating its assignment to 2nd *Chutai*. It also carried a nose-mounted 13 mm gun. Other *rikko* in

721 *Ku* were Model 24 *Tei* converted from Model 24 *Otsu*. which carried only a 7.7 mm gun in the nose. On those aircraft, the nose radar antenna was positioned at the tip of the nose cone glazing, rather than above.

30

G4M2E/MXY 7 721K-05 of Attack *Hikotai* 708/721 *Kokutai*, Usa Air Base, Kyushu, Japan, April 1945

Following participation in the Philippines campaign within 762 *Kokutai*, K708 returned to Japan. The *hikotai* was formally assigned to 721 *Ku* on 20 December 1944, and moved to Usa, in Kyushu, in 1945. It became the mainstay of 721 *Ku* after K711 was decimated on 21 March 1945, and between 1 April and 22 June undertook nine *Ohka* sorties. Unlike K711's flamboyant diagonal flash markings and three-digit individual aircraft numbers, K708 used just the letter 'K' and two-digit aircraft numbers to distinguish its aircraft from those of its sister *hikotai*.

31

Modified G4M2 3-*Ha* of Attack *Hikotai* 704/706 *Kokutai*, Yokosuka (Misawa) Air Base, Japan, August 1945

Many of the Type 1 *Rikko* intended for use in the *Tsurugi* commando raid on B-29 bases in the Marianas were specially modified with the dorsal turret removed and the opening faired over. This particular aircraft was photographed at Yokosuka shortly after the war, but would have been based at Misawa, in northern Honshu, for the operation. The number '3' on the tail indicated 3rd *Chutai*. For Operation *Tsurugi*, instead of an individual number, each aircraft was given a name, written in *kanji* characters, on the tail following the *chutai* number – in this case *Ha* means to 'break' or 'destroy'. Photo evidence indicates that aircraft earmarked for this operation also had their *hinomaru* painted out. 706 *Kokutai*, which would have been responsible for the aerial portion of Operation *Tsurugi*, was the last *rikko* unit formed by the IJN, being activated on 5 March 1945 at Kisarazu.

32

G4M2 951-1-363 of 951 *Kokutai*, Omura Detachment, Omura Air Base, Kyushu, Japan, June 1945

A limited number of Type 1 *Rikko* were assigned to anti-submarine patrol units towards the end of the war, with maritime *kokutai* being given numbers in the 900s range. The tail markings on this aircraft show a very rare example of a triangular presentation of the unit designator – the interceptor unit 352 *Ku* was the only outfit known to have used this style consistently. In the case of 951 *Ku*, the number '1' following the unit designator is believed to signify the Omura Detachment of the *kokutai*. As an anti-submarine patrol unit, 951 *Ku* operated several small detachments at various locations, Omura being the largest.

33

G6M1-L Z-985 (181) of the 1st *Kokutai*, South-east Asia, early 1942

One of the earliest G6M1s converted into a transport, this aircraft still displays an opening on the underside of the fuselage from where the ventral gondola of the original gunship had been removed. The individual aircraft number in the 900s range denotes a transport, and most interestingly, it has been painted over a number in the 100s range, which indicates a fighter. The latter almost certainly reflected its initial intended use as an escort gunship. The letter 'Z' was used by 1st *Kokutai* until November 1942. It flew Type 96 *Rikko* as a land attack unit, but also had a transport flight attached for paratroop operations during the opening months of the Pacific War.

34

G6M1-L P-911 of the Southeastern Area Fleet HQ, Lae, New Guinea, Summer 1943

The letter 'P' is believed to denote *Nanto Homen Kantai* (Southeastern Area Fleet) during the period in question, although the letter is also documented as having been used at one time by Southwestern Area Fleet. This aircraft was damaged and abandoned at Lae, New Guinea.

35

G6M1-L GF-2 of the Combined Fleet HQ, Haneda Airport, Tokyo, Japan, late 1943

This aircraft was used as a VIP transport, attached directly to the *Rengo Kantai* (Combined Fleet) HQ transport unit. Code letters 'GF' denoted *Rengo Kantai* at this time, but this was later changed to '160' when all-numerical codes were adopted.

36

G6M1-L X2-903 of 202 *Kokutai*, East Indies, Summer 1943

This aircraft was one of three transport hacks used by 202 *Kokutai*. Formerly 3rd *Kokutai*, it was the main fighter unit in the East Indies during 1943 – 'X' denoted the parent 23rd *Koku Sentai*. A characteristic of 202 *Kokutai* was that it was one of a minority of land-based units which painted its tail markings in red.

37

G4M2A 1022-81 (s/n 12142) of 1022 *Kokutai*, Lingayen, the Philippines, January 1945

By early 1945 the Type 1 *Rikko* was being used increasingly in the armed transport role, as it was deemed to be too vulnerable to operate as a land-based attack aircraft. 1022 *Ku* was formed on 10 July 1944. Most aircraft in transport units simply carried the last two digits of the unit number on their tails, but this is an unusual example in which all four digits are shown, followed by a two-digit individual aeroplane number.

38

G4M2A 81-926 of 1081 *Kokutai*, Atsugi Air Base, Japan, August 1945

1081 *Ku* was formed on 1 April 1944, and its aircraft sported a more typical tail marking style in which only the last two digits of the unit number were applied, followed by an individual aeroplane number in the 900s range. Highly unusual, however, is the stylised *Tsubame* (Swallow) marking painted on its aircraft – one of the rare examples of a pictorial unit marking in the IJN.

39
G4M3A 01-95 of 1001 *Kokutai*, Matsushima Air Base, Japan, July 1945
1001 *Kokutai* used the '01' unit code from September 1944 when it left Yokosuka Naval District and became a part of 101st *Koku Sentai*, under Combined Fleet. This aircraft is the only Model 34 so far known for which clear photographic evidence of unit markings exist. It is reported to have been drafted to serve as part of the second batch of aircraft collected for Operation *Tsurugi* following US carrier raids on northern Honshu bases on 14-15 July 1945. Unlike the original batch of aircraft prepared for the operation, there was no time to modify these replacement *rikko*. They also remained in the markings of their original units.

Back Cover Profile
G6M1-L 'Yo'A-987 of 1001 *Kokutai*, Kavieng, New Ireland, January 1944

Kokutai with numerical designations in the 1000s range denoted transport and ferry units. Activated on 1 July 1943 at Kisarazu, 1001 *Kokutai* was the first specialised air transport unit in the IJN, and was assigned directly to the Yokosuka Naval District. Its unit markings reflected this assignment, *Katakana* letter *Yo* (backward 'E') followed by 'A' indicating that 1001 *Ku* was the first unit assigned directly to Yokosuka Naval District. The *kokutai* undertook transport and ferrying duties throughout Japanese-occupied territory, and this particular aircraft was wrecked at Kavieng, New Ireland.

Back Cover Photo
The destroyer USS *Bagley* (DD-386) draws alongside a tailless Type 1 of 4th *Kokutai*, discovered floating in the water following the disastrous torpedo attack of 8 August 1942 off Guadalcanal. The *rikko* crew had survived the ditching and were sitting on the aeroplane's wing when the American destroyer approached. In a defiant gesture oft repeated during the Pacific War, these men fired their pistols at the ship, then turned the guns on themselves, rather than face capture (*Al Simmons Collection via Larry Hickey*)

SELECTED BIBLIOGRAPHY

Iwaya Fumio. *Chuko*. Hara Shobo, 1976

Izawa Yasuho. *Rikko To Ginga*. Asahi Sonorama, 1995

Chukokai. *Kaigun Chuko Shiwa Shu*. Privately Published, 1980

Kaigun 705. *Ku Kai Dai 705 Kaigun Kokutai Shi*. Privately Published, 1975

Kaiku. *Kai Umiwashi No Koseki*. Hara Shobo, 1982

Ikari Yoshiro. *Kaigun Kugisho*. Kojinsha, 1989

Sudo Hajime. *Malay Oki Kaisen*. Shiragane Shobo, 1974

Sekine Seiji. *Hono-o No Tsubasa*. Konnichi-no-Wadaisha, 1976

Takahashi Shosaku et. al. *Kaigun Rikujo Kogeki-Ki Tai*. Konnichi-no-Wadaisha, 1976

Murakami Masuo. *Shito No Ozora*. Asahi Sonorama, 1984

Kuramasu Jitsuyoshi. *Bokyo No Senki*. Kojinsha, 1987

Inoue Shoji. *Ichi Shiki Rikko Raigeki Ki*. Kojinsha, 1998

Boeicho Boeikenshusho Senshishitsu. *Senshi Sosho (Various Volumes)*. Asagumo Shimbunsha, 1969 etc.

Lundstrom, John B. *The First Team*. Naval Institute Press, 1984

Lundstrom, John B. *The First Team and the Guadalcanal Campaign*. Naval Institute Press, 1994

Shores, Christopher et. al. *Bloody Shambles Vol. 1*. Grub Street, 1992

Shores, Christopher et. al. *Bloody Shambles Vol. 2*. Grub Street, 1993

Bartsch, William H. *Doomed at the Start*. Texas A&M University Press, 1992

Tillman, Barrett. *Hellcat*. Naval Institute Press, 1979

Boer, P C. *De Luchtstrijd rond Borneo*. Van Holkema & Warendorf, 1987

Boer, P C. *De Luchtstrijd om Indie*. Van Holkema & Warendorf, 1990

Hickey, Lawrence J. *Warpath Across the Pacific, 4th Revised Ed. (Eagles over the Pacific. Vol. 1)*. International Research and Publishing, 1996

INDEX

References to illustrations are shown in **bold**.
Plates are shown with page and caption locators in brackets.